SOLD!

THE AUTOBIOGRAPHY OF
CHARLIE ROSS

WITH STEWART ROSS

BB
BLEAN BOOKS

First published 2024 by Blean Books

Westfield, Blean, Kent CT2 9ER

www.bleanbooks.co.uk

Copyright © 2024 Charlie Ross, Stewart Ross

The authors' moral rights are hereby asserted.

ISBN 978-0-9571019-4-4 (hbk)

A CIP catalogue for this book is available from the British Library.

All rights reserved. No part of this publication may be reproduced in any form or by any means (including photocopying or storing it in any medium by electronic means or whether or not transiently or incidentally to some other use of this publication) without the written permission of the copyright owner.

Printed and bound by CPI Group (UK) Ltd, Croydon, CR0 4YY

Acknowledgements

This book would not have been completed without the constant badgering (and help) of my wife Sally, the supreme literary skills of my brother Stewart and the painstaking professional proofreading of my sister-in-law Lucy.

Thanks must also go to my designer and the website supremo, Ed Ludlow.

Finally, I am most grateful to all those who have spoken kindly of my story as well as the good folk mentioned in this book who have – wittingly or unwittingly – helped me along my journey.

CONTENTS

List of Illustrations vii

1. *Put Another Nickel in* 11
2. *An Education – of a Sort* 19
3. *Cars, Chickens and a Clock* 27
4. *Starting with Spraggs* 43
5. *Bread and Butter* 57
6. *Plimsolls* 69
7. *Downer Ross* 79
8. *Clearing Houses* 95
9. *Che Sara Sara* 107
10. *For I am a Pirate King!* 123
11. *Elyot's Nose* 133
12. *Flogging It!* 151
13. *Road Trips* 161
14. *Howzat!* 175
15. *By Elephant to the Subcontinent* 189
16. *Hunting Bargains* 199
17. *An Alien of Extraordinary Ability* 207
18. *Putters and Punters* 219
19. *Boxers and Beetles* 233
20. *Six of the Best* 245

To Finn, Max, Ana and Zac ...
I'm looking forward to handing over the gavel to one of you!

List of Illustrations

1. Safe in the arms of my big brother, 1951.
2. My father and I on Climping Beach, 1951.
3. Stewart (the large one) and I in Berkhamsted School uniform, c.1964.
4. First taste of greasepaint: as Ford in a 1967 school production of *The Merry Wives of Windsor*.
5. Berkhamsted School 1st X1 (cricket), 1967.
6. Buckingham Rugby Club Exiles XV, 1983.
7. Astonishingly, the Richard Ellis team won the 1972 RICS 7-a-side Rugby Tournament.
8. Panto time: Widow Wonkey in Bicester Choral & Operatic Society's production of *The Magic Lamp*, 2012.
9. As Professor Higgins in Bicester Choral & Operatic Society's *My Fair Lady*, with son Olly as Freddy Eynsford-Hill & Kerry Ayers as Eliza Doolittle, 2005.
10. Auctioneer in disguise: playing Fagin in Bicester Choral & Operatic Society's production of *Oliver!*, 2004.
11. The Pirate King carries off his loot in Oxford Operatic Society's *The Pirates of Penzance*, 1998.
12. At a charity event, 1985. The charismatic lady needs no introduction.
13. The Downer Ross auction room, Woburn.
14. The magnificent Anglo-Indian Partner's Desk at the heart of my Nottingham adventure.
15 and 16. A George Bullock sofa, bought for £190, painstakingly restored, and eventually sold for £32,000 – before and after restoration.

17. The sumptuous collection of Canalettos at Woburn Abbey © courtesy of The Woburn Abbey Collection.
18. Liz Zettl, famous in the office for her unorthodox operation of the space bar, and subsequently a character in the BBC drama *The Sixth Commandment*, 2023.
19. Any further bids? Auctioneering in the Woburn saleroom, c.1990.
20. Tea for two: Christina Trevanion and I enjoying a *Road Trip* in the Scottish Highlands, 2014 © courtesy of STV.
21. Doing my best James Bond impersonation, with Honor Blackman in *Celebrity Antiques Road Trip*, 2012 © courtesy of STV.
22. Doing time for *Bargain Hunt*, 2019 © courtesy of the BBC.
23. The Staffordshire Indian Elephant that carried me into the national newspapers, *Antiques Road Trip*, 2012.
24. James Braxton and I about to brave the freezing North Sea for *Antiques Road Trip*, 2012 © courtesy of STV.
25. Our youthful Executive Producer, Paul Tucker, Caroline Quentin, Terry Wogan and me relaxing during the filming of an episode of *Celebrity Antiques Road Trip* © courtesy of STV.
26. The locking mechanism on an Armada Chest of the type that got me into hot water during my first appearance on *Antiques Roadshow*.
27. I learned more history on *Antiques Road Trip* than I ever did at school. On a visit to Northampton, I learned of the remarkable career of Walter Tull, pioneering Afro-Caribbean footballer and soldier © courtesy of The Finlayson Family Archive.
28. The things I do for *Bargain Hunt* … bubble bath, 2023 © courtesy of the BBC.
29. With Jarvis Cocker, Bez, Rowetta Idah and Candida Doyle

during the "cheating" episode of *Bargain Hunt* © courtesy of the BBC.
30. High kicks from the *Bargain Hunt* red and blue teams, with Philip Serrell and Thomas Forrester – and my MCC braces! © courtesy of the BBC.
31. The *Bargain Hunt* Rocker © courtesy of the BBC.
32. With fellow rock stars Philip Serrell, Charles Hanson and James Braxton in the Saga Entertainment Christmas Song, 2017.
33. My normal footwear is rather conservative but for The Honeypot Children's Charity auction I was most elegantly shod, courtesy of Sir Elton John!
34. Panting for Sands (Stillbirth and Neonatal Death Charity) during the Great North Run, September 2013.
35. Enjoying myself hugely as the "View from the Boundary" guest on Test Match Special, 2022 (Radio 5 Sports Extra).
36. Serious business with the Lord's Taverners Cricket XI: Chris Tarrant and I discuss tactics.
37. Going, going … knocking down a rare Duesenberg at Pebble Beach, 2018. It fetched a record $22M © courtesy of Gooding & Company – photo by Mathieu Heurtault.
38. Covid or not, the show must go on at the Gooding & Company auction in Hampton Court, 2020 © courtesy of Gooding & Company.
39. Offscreen and onto stage with Philip Serrell and Christina Trevanion on our *Antiques and a Little Bit of Nonsense* theatre tour, 2023–2024.
40. No Gooding & Company auction would be complete without a starring performance from Sally, aka Lady Ross! © courtesy of Gooding & Company – photo by Hanna Yamamoto.
41. Sally and I on our wedding day, July 30 1977.

42. The Ross/Macdonald Clan, Easter 2024.
43. 1935 Duesenberg SJ Speedster – the Mormon Meteor © courtesy of Gooding & Company.
44. Austin-Healey 3000 MK111 BJ8 © courtesy of Gooding & Company – photo by Josh Hway.
45. Bugatti Type 59 Sports © courtesy of Gooding & Company – photo by Mathieu Heurtault.
46. Though the Hillman Husky was not the grandest of cars, it will always hold a special place in my affections for the golden memories it inspired.
47. Mercedes Simplex 60 hp © courtesy of Gooding & Company – photo by Mathieu Heurtault.
48. The Vespa 125 was my teenage passport to a brave new world, 1967.

Front cover – Auctioning at Pebble Beach © courtesy of Gooding & Company.

Inside dust jacket – 1938 Bugatti Type 57C Aravis 'Special Cabriolet' © courtesy of Gooding & Company. Image by Brian Henniker. Sold for $6,605,000, 2024.

Back cover – The famous Staffordshire Indian Elephant, 2012 © courtesy of STV.

CHAPTER ONE

Put Another Nickel in

The beginning is, I suppose, as good a place to start as any.

We are in Aylesbury, Bucks (where the ducks come from) on a warm Thursday afternoon in late June 1950. Elsewhere, memorable events are unfolding. President Truman is explaining to the world that he is authorising what he calls a "police action" in Korea, in the soccer World Cup the American team is defeating the country that invented the modern game, and – of much greater interest to me – the West Indies cricket team are romping to a ground-breaking 326-run victory over Freddie Brown's England.

Nearer to home, outside the maternity wing of the Royal Bucks Hospital, an itinerant musician is playing the hurdy-gurdy and singing,

> *Put another nickel in*
> *In the nickelodeon*
> *All I want is loving you*
> *And music, music, music*

Inside, my mother is giving birth to me. The business done, she takes one look at her baby and pronounces with customary conviction, 'This child will be a ballet dancer!'

Wrong. As it turned out, the hurdy-gurdy man's foreshadowing was much closer to the mark. Both he and my mother got the music bit right – all my life I have been an enthusiastic and moderately tuneful singer in bath and on stage – but only the twanger outside my mother's window got the money bit right, though "nickel" turned out to be a bit of an understatement.

Fifty-four years have passed, and we have crossed the Atlantic to an enormous, specially erected marquee at Pebble Beach, California. We are at the inaugural Gooding & Company car auction, a brand that will shortly become world-famous.

I am seated (one of the few auctions I conduct from a chair), glasses on nose, gavel in hand, on the smart blue podium. Beside me sits David Gooding, courteous, calm and unquestionably collected. Before me, seated and standing, is an audience of around two thousand, among whom are some of the wealthiest men and women in America. Impeccable manners, razor-sharp minds. To my left crouches a great beast of a motor car, the yellow Duesenberg Mormon Meteor: in 1935, its gigantic 420 cubic inch, supercharged 8-cylinder engine had enabled it to set a new world record by averaging 153.823 mph over a single twenty-four-hour period. Stationary at the moment, but very much part of the show.

I suppose I ought to be nervous, but I'm not. It's all far too fast-moving and exciting to reflect on what's going on. Adrenalin and the quick wit inherited from my father run the show. It's not unlike being in a play or musical; the main difference is that you don't have to learn any words – you just make up the lines as you go along.

On this occasion they come easily because I'd used them

many, many times before. The numbers, however, are not quite the same – Gooding & Company do not deal in nickels.

As in all good auctions, the tension is building nicely. Some of those seeking to purchase the yellow monster have travelled to Pebble Beach to be present in person. Three individuals catch my eye. One is a large man wearing a flamboyant (to British eyes) cowboy hat; he appears to be sweating rather profusely and he signals bids with a wave of the eight-inch cigar held between the podgy fingers of his right hand. The second is an elegant lady in an immaculately cut black suit seated near the front; she contacts me with knowing looks and the faintest of nods. The third, and most noticeable, is a trim middle-aged gentleman who appears too excited to stand still; strolling about the marquee with a mobile phone clamped to his ear, he gallantly waves his free hand whenever the bid is raised.

Anonymity heightens the drama. As well as bidders on the floor, a bank of discreet operators is taking phone bids from callers whose identity is not disclosed.

Once we have passed the $2 million mark, the number of bidders falls away quite quickly. One by one, the telephone operators hang up. The lady in the suit smiles and stops nodding. At $3 million, the cowboy drops out with a muffled oath of annoyance. As he mops his brow with an enormous yellow handkerchief, I wonder whether he had bought it specially to match his planned acquisition. Oh vanity! An auction can be a cruel occasion.

There are now two people left, one on the phone and the trim stroller. The audience is warming to their local hero. Every time he bids, the crowd cheers. When he is topped by the phone caller, the marquee groans. Can the figure on the other end of the line hear? If they can, then it is spurring them on, for we are now approaching an astonishing $4 million. Both bidders are still with me.

I'm enjoying this!

The cheers and groans continue a little longer until, finally, the groans have it. The chap in the marquee drops out to sympathetic cries of 'well done!' and the phone bidder – anonymous to the last – stands on the verge of victory.

'For the first time at 4.05 million,' I call. 'For the second time at 4.05 million … For the third and last time at 4.05 million dollars!'

Total and absolute silence. Like being in space, I imagine. The usual cliché is that you can hear a pin drop; on this occasion, a falling feather would have resounded like a thunderclap.

I look around at the sea of rapt faces. Any last-minute hiccups? No. That's it. I raise my gavel.

'Make no mistake, I'm selling.'

The silence is getting oppressive. Down comes the gavel – bang! Sold!

It takes about a second for the impact of what has happened to sink in before the crowd bursts into a cacophony of clapping punctuated by the occasional all-American hoot of approval. The vehicle that had set one world speed record has now (2004) set another: the most expensive American car ever sold.

I was glad I hadn't gone into ballet!

As much as anything, luck had carried me to that exalted podium. A few months previously, I had been chatting to Peter Bainbridge, a friend who at the time ran an auction house in Ruislip.

One afternoon, as we were discussing the sad fall in the value of antique dark wood furniture, he remarked casually,

'I've just come back from the States, Charlie.'

'Hols? You must be making too much money.'

'Ha-ha! No, I was over there doing a bit of vintage car auctioning. Mentioned you, actually.'

'Me? What for?'

'David Gooding, a guy I had worked with over there, is setting up his own auction in Pebble Beach, California. He told me he needs a top-class auctioneer …'

'And?'

'I said I know this old bald chap in Woburn; he's quite witty and always on the lookout for something out of the ordinary –'

'Thanks Peter. You couldn't be more flattering if you tried.'

'No, seriously Charlie, I reckon you and David would get on pretty well.'

And we did.

Not long afterwards, David flew over to England to run his eye over a collection of old cars and check out whether any of them would be suitable for his upcoming auction. There weren't. He was looking for historic Bentleys with original upholstery, not rusty MGBs with bald tyres and 140,000 on the clock. Well, if the cars were no good, what about the chap from Woburn whom Peter Bainbridge had mentioned – the one with a receding hair line and a quick wit?

David duly called me and we arranged to meet at the Randolph Hotel in Oxford, the five-star pile of Victorian Gothic on the corner of Beaumont Street and Magdalen Street where Inspector Morse liked to down his pints. As I do on important occasions, I asked my wife Sally to accompany me. I was hoping that her good looks and charm would counterbalance the somewhat enigmatic portrait of me painted by Peter Bainbridge.

My heart sank when David came down the hotel stairs. I should have done my homework. Instead of the anticipated elderly tycoon with swelling tummy and watery eye, in strode a sleek young man half my age. Oh Lord! If I was expected to know about Coldplay and Kanye West rather than Gilbert and Sullivan, this was not going to end well.

Happily, my fears were misplaced. Sally and I invited David to dinner at Gees Restaurant, where we enjoyed Mediterranean food in a Victorian glasshouse. As the evening wore on, Sally and I became increasingly taken with our guest. His manners, as with all Americans of his ilk, were immaculate. He was patently honest and knew an inordinate amount about everything – even Gilbert and Sullivan. He said kind things about my range of auctioneering experience, including my TV work, and even seemed impressed that I had played the Pirate King in *The Pirates of Penzance* at the Oxford Playhouse.

I'm not sure what he made of my knowledge of vintage motor cars. By dredging from a hazy memory the names of Dinky Toys we had once collected (Vanwall, 'D' Type, etc) and the stately vehicle (Bentley) kept in the garage by the father of one of my brother's girlfriends, I hoped to give the impression of knowing more than I actually did. I also announced with great pride that in the 1930s my father (more of whom later) had once raced from John O'Groats to Land's End in his home-made "Ross Special".

'Did he win, Charlie?'

'Actually, I'm not sure. But knowing my father, he almost certainly didn't.'

'Broke down?'

'Everything he did broke down.'

David smiled – and I liked him even more. I don't have much time for people without a sense of humour. He assured me that the cars he would be selling never broke down, especially when they cost hundreds of thousands, even millions, of dollars.

Millions of dollars? I thought. *You could buy my Woburn saleroom several times over for that, with the contents thrown in.*

At the end of the meal, David said he would be in touch. In the meantime, would I send him a show reel? Hoping that he didn't mean a film of me Highland dancing in my kilt, I put together some shots from the *Antiques Road Show* and *Flog It!* and rounded them off with a couple of minutes of me prancing about before tipsy punters at a charity dinner auction.

The combination of Sally, the dinner and the video clips did the trick. A few days later I received an email:

I would like you, Charlie, to conduct my first sale at Pebble Beach in August.

I gulped. I hadn't yet had the courage to tell him that, (a) I'd never been to America; (b) I'd never sold anything in dollars, and (c) I'd certainly never sold anything for anywhere near a million anythings, or even quarter of a million, or even 100,000!

Why not? I asked myself. *I'll give it a try. In for a nickel, in for a dollar.*

Talking of dollars, David asked what my fee would be. 'Thank you, David,' I replied. 'Please fly me out business class and put me up at a nice hotel. I will then conduct your sale and return home. After that, pay me what you think I'm worth.'

It was a bit of a gamble, but as I was convinced David was a straightforward decent guy there wasn't much to lose. And much to gain: a comfy flight to a new continent, a week or so in a lovely part of the world with charming hosts, and a crash course in some of the most stunning pieces of machinery ever made.

As you may have guessed, David did not let me down. In fact, he paid me more than I would have charged had I sent an invoice. And during my stay we struck up a strong and enduring friendship. It was he who was kind enough to call me "the world's greatest auctioneer" – a nifty bit of marketing, of course, rather than a statement of fact. Nevertheless, since that day I have conducted all but one of his vintage car auctions (I missed one in 2022 with a detached retina), and nearly every car he has sold has come under my hammer. Their total price was once estimated to be well over $1 billion. It's now definitely north of $2 billion.

Sometimes, as I gaze about me from the suave blue podium of a Gooding & Company auction, I find it hard to take in. In my mind's eye I return to where it all began. My first lot, as a gawky eighteen-year-old, was a pen of chickens at Bletchley Market. On that occasion, I had proudly brought the hammer down at three shillings and six pence (17.5p). And now …

I've worked hard, yes. But I have also been very, very fortunate.

CHAPTER TWO

An Education – of a Sort

My parents were nomads. If this conjures up romantic images of a scruffy but smiling little Charlie seated on a gaily painted caravan harnessed to a sleepy dobbin, forget it. We zig-zagged from house to house around Bedfordshire and North Buckinghamshire because that's where my father's employment circus took us. The only fixed point in our domestic perambulations was my mother's job at the Red Cross physiotherapy clinic in Bletchley, where she worked first as a member of staff (under the oddly named Mr Diddums) then as head of department. She was the white-coated, unflinchingly efficient and successful hub of our family life. Her sun-like gravity held my brother Stewart and me in orbit while my father, like a domestic Pluto, circled distantly on the edge of our solar system before eventually spinning off into a universe of his own.

'Education' Albert Einstein is supposed to have said, 'is what remains after one has forgotten what one has learned in school.' As you will soon discover, I learned very little at school, apart from a ridiculous school song (in Latin) and the laws of cricket and rugby – so there wasn't much to forget.

True to Einstein's dictum, my principal education came from what went on at home in the form of parental influence and example. My mother first.

Marjorie Eleanor Ross (née Bliss) was a highly intelligent, staggeringly diligent, warm-hearted snob. In her youth she had dreamed of being a doctor but when her civil servant father (bowler-hatted commuter to the Inland Revenue) considered this unsuitable work for a young woman, she had to make do with physiotherapy. She also dreamed of being a sheepskin-coated lady of leisure serving smoked salmon sandwiches from the back of a Volvo in the West car park of Twickenham rugby football ground. When my father's failure to bring in sufficient income disabled her from this role, or any other role that brought the social status she craved, she compensated by working like a trojan and developing an increasingly bitter scorn for her husband. The lessons this taught me? Marry wisely, work hard, and try not to take anything too seriously, especially life.

Graham Stewart Ross, my father, was in many ways the perfect gentleman (though an out-dated phrase, I think we all know what it means). My mother married him for his excellent manners, dashing good looks, quick mind, and delightful sense of humour. What more could a wife ask for? Well, for a dyslexic with no professional qualifications, a sound business sense would have come in handy. He passed his youth spending his father's money and rallying in his aforementioned "Ross Special" car. After marriage and war service in the RAF, he tried his hand, successively but never successfully, at pest control, farm management (twice), pig raising, chicken and duck production, grocery supervision for Fine Fare supermarkets, running his own Vespa sales and service business, and finally selling sweets, cigarettes and sandwiches from a small shop in Dunstable Place, Luton. When this finally went bust in his third bankruptcy, so did he. The lesson this taught me was a great deal more useful than the school song. It was, in the words of Wilkins Micawber in *David Copperfield*, 'Annual income twenty pounds, annual expenditure nineteen pounds, nineteen and six, result happiness. Annual income twenty pounds, annual expenditure twenty pounds ought and six, result misery.' I have never forgotten it.

A third family member had a considerable influence on me while I was growing up. "Uncle Mac", my father's elder brother, was one of the country's most successful (and wealthy) dentists. The private patients who made their way over the plush carpets of his lavish practice at 19a Cavendish Square, between Harley Street and Oxford Street, included film star Anna Neagle, top BBC commentator Raymond Glendenning, and no less a personage than the Prime Minister himself, the Rt Hon Sir Winston Churchill. Mac's natural charm and good manners made them all feel comfortable, whatever procedure they were being subjected to.

Owing to the Ross family's eccentric and sometimes didactic system of nomenclature, Mac was not McAnything but Wallace Stewart Ross, his first name honouring the Scottish patriot of recent cinematographic fame. Mac's father (William Wallace Ross) was always "Chief" (ie head of the clan) and *his* father, William Stewart Ross, was "Saladin" (scourge of the Christians), the pseudonym he used as a prominent freethinking polemicist. Chief, my grandfather, preordained my name by calling for a toast to 'Charlie Ross' while I was still in my mother's womb. When it came to choosing names for our children, my wife Sally decided it was time to end this sentimental faux-Scottishness, though it continued for another generation in my brother's family.

For our family, a visit from Uncle Mac was a state occasion. First, the roar of the Jaguar Mark II 3.4 outside the front door, then the presents, the jokes, the stories and on departure the ten-shilling note discreetly pressed into my palm with his farewell handshake. Even better were visits to London to have my teeth checked in his plush practice. How my Clarks winklepickers sank into the soft pile beneath my feet! How subtle was the solid tick of the 18th-century longcase clock that stood sentry beside the Gillows sideboard! How heart-melting were the smiles of the super-attractive nurses as they took my coat and ushered me into the presence of the great Doctor Ross! After the gentlest of repairs to my teeth, from the age of sixteen onwards Mac invariably took me out to dinner at the Hunting Lodge, a top-end Regent Street restaurant. A sumptuous dinner of smoked salmon and fillet steak was followed by a further treat: a spin at roulette in The Palm Beach Club in Berkeley Street. I handed over a cheque for £5 and Mac passed me the equivalent in gaming chips. Not once did he cash the cheque.

Beautiful things, beautiful people, beautiful surroundings …. The contrast with my father's converted bakery where he repaired scooters was painful. I wanted to live like Uncle Mac, and I knew how to do it. I would become a dentist.

At this point I need to rewind a little. Unlike my father, who as far as I know had almost no schooling, I was summoned by bells between the ages of five and eighteen. The call started at Stoke Hammond Village School, where I was good at sums. At the age of seven, I was sent away to boarding school in Berkhamsted. Two questions come to mind: how and why?

The first is easily answered. How did the parents who turned up in a nicotine-stained Hillman Husky afford to pay the same fees as those sweeping up the drive in their Riley Pathfinders? By borrowing, of course. When the extent of my father's loans was finally revealed the year after I left school, the spectrum of debtors was extraordinary. It ranged from finance companies to neighbours and the family doctor. He had even persuaded the lady who served in his sweet shop to hand over her life's savings. All but the latter, I imagine, bailed him out in order to support my mother, whom they adored, rather than with any hope of repayment. My hero Uncle Mac never borrowed a penny.

And why private boarding education, which was beyond our means? The answer lay with my mother, who made all the important family decisions. She always maintained she sent her children to boarding school so they would come under the influence of "professionals", men who knew what was best for young boys – a clear vote of no confidence in my father. Given the shambolic amateurishness, even incompetence, of many who taught me, this explanation hardly bears scrutiny. The real reason she sent us away was twofold: so she could focus on her work, which she loved, and because of the kudos in the social circles to which she aspired of having "the boys away at school". Incidentally, I was not sent to the same prep school as my brother, Stewart. The Dragon School, Oxford, was regarded as too tough for me as I was a feeble, weak-chested child who had to be wrapped in Guernsey sweaters and taken off to Polperro, Cornwall, to be beefed up by bracing sea air. When handling 100 auction lots in six hours non-stop in America, I sometimes wonder about that "weak chest" diagnosis. The only authenticated illness I suffered from as a child was a very mild case of polio.

As this is meant to be a light-hearted peep behind the curtain of my professional life, I won't waste much time on my schooldays. I enjoyed sport, singing and drama, none of which bore much relation to my putative career as a dentist. As things turned out, acting in plays offered a useful grounding for rostrum work. My starring role was probably Ford in Shakespeare's *The Merry Wives of Windsor*: the school magazine was kind enough to say I "attacked the lines with style and gusto." All I recall was belting furiously around the stage yelling 'Buck! Buck! Buck!' and wishing I had the guts to change that initial letter!

Three memories remain from my time at prep school, two of which are unpleasant. One is of the sadistic pleasure my housemaster took in beating little boys on the bottom with a cane. The misdemeanour was irrelevant: being late for something, talking when one was not supposed to, not learning Latin verbs – they all meant a summons to the study and the chilling command 'bend over'. A most sinister ritual followed. Mr Evans – I've changed the name lest any of the pupils' surviving relatives are incited to desecrate his grave – offered the first few words of explanation of what was happening (eg 'This, Ross, is for talking …'), raised the cup of tea he always brought with him for the ceremony, took a sip, and thwacked the victim's backside with the cane. He then continued with the explanation ('… in the dormitory …'), took another sip of tea, and delivered the second blow. And so it went on until the tea and explanation were finished, and the poor child on the receiving end was wincing in pain and doing their best not to blub. I'm not sure if I remember this correctly, but I seem to recall that one was expected to whisper, 'Thank you, sir,' before creeping from the room. Nowadays, thank God, men like Evans are locked up.

My second prep school memory is not mine but Stewart's. At the back of my boarding house was an asphalt playground surrounded by wire fencing. It overlooked Chesham Road along which Stewart, then at Berkhamsted senior school, passed every day on his way to and from his boarding house. Whenever possible, I ran up to the wire and exchanged a few words with him. Talking to the thin, sad-eyed little boy on the other side of the fence was, he says, like a scene from *Oliver Twist*. My happy memories of the time were Sunday afternoons, when the two of us were allowed to go out for a walk together. I forget what we talked about – conkers, probably – but I do recall the fun we had tuning in on a transistor radio to *Round the Horn* and *The Navy Lark*. Has British radio comedy ever been better?

As you may have noticed, so far I've avoided talking about the academic side of school life. It started out OK. I was accepted into the senior school and did well at O-Levels: the gleaming black door of 19a Cavendish Square was coming nicely into focus. It was – alas! – a mirage. My O-Level results should have given sufficient warning of what rapids lay ahead, for my best grades were in French, English and maths. Entry into medical school to study dentistry required A-Levels in physics, chemistry and biology.

For my final two years at school I was quite well taught. Biology was effectively imparted by George Grace, a genial man who became famous throughout the school for rebuking a boy telling a dirty joke with a phrase: 'Good Lord, Smith [or whatever his name was], that's not only not funny, it's also biologically impossible.' P.V.C. Williams was our excellent, friendly chemistry master. His real name was S.P.C. Williams, but it was rumoured that while working for Kodak he had blown himself up and had received extensive plastic surgery. Schoolboy nicknames can be very cruel. So can life – I heard later that P.V.C. had taken his own, as did my inspiring and Wilde-like English teacher, Brian Terry. I don't remember who taught me physics. They were probably OK, but I was not a good pupil. I didn't understand much of all that heat, light and sound stuff: only later in life did it dawn on me that the Watt who invented the steam engine had nothing whatsoever to do with the brightness of a light bulb.

There were eight in my sixth-form science class, all hoping for a career in some form of medicine. In the autumn of 1967, we filled in our UCCA forms for entry to medical school and waited anxiously for the response. In those days

A-Level pass grades ranged from A to E, and my seven contemporaries were offered places conditional on their getting a mix of As and Bs. To their astonishment, Ross, C.G. did rather better.

I was interviewed at six London hospitals, including King's College, University College, Guy's, and St George's. Unknown to the school, my inspiration, Uncle Mac, had had a quiet word with each of them beforehand and they all duly obliged him by offering me a place to study dentistry as long as I passed the requisite three A-Levels – yes, pass. All I needed were three Es.

You can guess what happened, can't you? Seven of the eight applying for medical school achieved the necessary grades and were admitted. The eighth failed all his exams and was accordingly rejected. I was that eighth man. As no one understood what had happened, it was suggested I repeat a year and sit the exams again. Surely next time … ? The offer was withdrawn when my father's cheque for the summer term's fees bounced.

I left school feeling rather miserable. My mother consulted her library of blue Pelican books on psychology, sociology, adolescence, etc, and came up with a semi-scientific explanation for my state of mind and what had happened. I don't think it was very accurate. Except when singing, on stage or playing field, I was pretty miserable throughout my school career. I had never been able to accept a regime where a lop-eared, beak-nosed idiot of a house tutor punished me for being late back one evening after my father had had a puncture, and where Stewart was reprimanded for talking to me – his brother, for goodness' sake! – simply because I was two years junior to him. No, classrooms, exams and petty rules were just not my scene.

It was now up to me to find out what was.

CHAPTER THREE

Cars, Chickens and a Clock

If at the time someone had told me that my A-Level debacle was the best thing that could have happened to me, I wouldn't have believed them. I had wanted to be a dentist, hadn't I? And that path was now closed. But was dentistry what I truly hankered after? Though no scholar, I am good with figures and perfectly capable of remembering what is important to me. If I had really, really wanted to spend my life yanking at other people's molars, wouldn't I have managed, by hook or by crook, to get those three Es?

I'm not suggesting for one minute that I failed my A-Levels deliberately, I simply wasn't motivated. I didn't dream of drills – they were a means to an end. I had been attracted to Uncle Mac's practice in 19a Cavendish Square not by the dentures, even though they had belonged to Winston Churchill, but by the mahogany elegance of the Gillows sideboard, the subtle workmanship of the longcase clock, and the sleek lines of the Jaguar Mark II 3.4 garaged nearby. Somewhere deep inside me lay a secret desire to be involved with art. I also needed to interact with whole people, not just their teeth.

On finishing at boarding school, I lived with my mother in Great Brickhill, a village that overlooked the flat farmland that would shortly be swallowed up by the new city of Milton Keynes. The only work available in our village was either serving in The Old Red Lion or farm labouring. As neither offered much in the way of a career, to get a moderately well-paid job I had to venture down the hill to Bletchley. Nowadays, because we know what had gone on at Bletchley Park during the Second World War, a pink cloud of thrilling nostalgia hangs over this ugly railway town. When I lived nearby, nobody even knew of the existence of the park – at least, a few must have done but they never mentioned it. Certainly not Bimbo Norman, a professor of Medieval German from London University and friend of my parents who lived in nearby Bow Brickhill. At the time, I wondered vaguely why anyone working in London would choose to live there. It turned out that he had moved near Bletchley in 1939 when the government requisitioned his expertise in regional German accents and he stayed when the war ended.

The professor's activities in Bletchley were rather different from mine. While he had helped decide the fate of nations in top secret, I ended up helping decide the fate of chickens in Bletchley Market. For this – and it turned out more fortunate than it might sound – I had my mother to thank. Because of her fine work with the Red Cross and through her extensive network of private patients (she always hoped the Duke of Bedford would give her a Canaletto as a tip for her services), she was a well-known and highly respected member of the community. As a consequence, she had no difficulty lining up a couple of job interviews for me.

The first was with Associated Octel, a science-based company with a factory in Bletchley that specialised (I think) in removing lead from petrol. For some extraordinary reason, my interviewer thought that my RP accent and polite manner, combined with the fact that I had done three sciences at A-Level (ahem!), made me a suitable prospect, and he offered me a job at a handsome salary. I hesitated.

My second interview was with W.S. Johnson & Co, a respected local firm of land and estate agents. I checked out what they did. Like many firms of chartered surveyors back in 1968, they sold houses, farms, livestock, factories, and the entire contents of houses whose owners had died, gone bankrupt, or met with some other misfortune. Houses interested me a bit, certainly a lot more than farms and factories, and my enthusiasm for livestock was even less than that for physics. I don't think I could have distinguished between a Jersey Red and a Jersey Royal. But house contents were a different matter altogether ... Might there possibly be, nestling in a dusty corner and not wound up for fifty years, an 18th-century longcase clock?

My interview with Dick Arnold, the senior partner of W.S. Johnson & Co, was unusual. He was a tall man with a bushy moustache, two protruding top front teeth and a genial, no-nonsense manner that went down well with farmers. With his cloth cap perched at a sporty angle and referring to everyone – man, woman, child and animal – as "old boy", he was in his element selling cattle and sheep in Bletchley Market. My interview with him concluded thus:

'Charlie, old boy, if you join us – and I hope you will – we'll put you on to selling houses. And Charlie, old boy, you sell one a day. And Charlie, old boy, if you can't sell one a day, then you sell one a week. And Charlie, old boy, if you can't sell one a week, then you sell one a month.'

'Will that be all, Mr Arnold?'

'No, Charlie, old boy. If you can't sell one a month, you'd better bugger off!'

I took the job.

W.S. Johnson & Co had been founded by William Spencer Johnson, known among senior members of the firm as "Spen". He was a short, brusque man in his late 60s, stubby in stature and manner. One of my jobs was to buy his daily packet of Albany cigarettes. With "F.L. Smith, Burlington Gardens, Old Bond Street" on the face of the packet, they were a rung above the average Player's Navy Cut or Wills's Woodbine and retailed for one shilling and ten pence a packet – about what a farm labourer earned in an hour. Spen didn't trust me with a two-shilling coin (aka a "florin"). Each morning, I had to ask Miss Jenkins, the diminutive cashier whose legs resembled those of a Victorian cabriole, for the exact money: a one-shilling coin (aka a "bob"), a sixpenny bit, a thruppenny bit and a large bronze-coloured penny. Three years later, this bizarre system of pounds, shillings and pence, not to mention guineas and ten-bob notes, was swept away by the arrival of decimal currency – and people complained!

My guide and mentor during my early years at W.S. Johnson & Co was Spen's son, David. A quiet, intense young man, he inherited his formidable father's money but not his business acumen. David's passion was for motor cars, and, by his early thirties, he had built up an impressive collection that included a Rolls-Royce Phantom II, an Aston Martin DB4, a Lagonda that I believe had won the Le Mans 24-hour race in 1935, and a chain-driven Frazer Nash. When I auction gleaming, immaculate examples of cars like these at Gooding & Company, Pebble Beach, California, I am taken back to the barn in Shenley Church End (now a suburb of Milton Keynes) where David kept his collection, and wonder what has happened to it and what, if the vehicles were lovingly burnished like their American siblings, they would be worth. Certainly many, many millions.

I think David saw me more as a companion than an apprentice, someone with whom he could chat about cars and motoring rather than about profit and loss and the price of pigs. On my first day at work, he said, quite out of the blue, 'I have to go to Newport Pagnell to collect the P2 this afternoon. Would you mind coming with me?'

P2? Was this some sort of tax office form, like a P45? Not wishing to display my ignorance, I said I'd be happy to accompany him. I followed him downstairs to the car park and walked towards the second car I had owned, a blue Morris Minor Mini van.

'No, sorry, Charlie. We'll go in mine. You'll need to be driving back.'

His was the Aston Martin DB4. Four decades later, when auctioning one of these cars in America, the feeling of awe as I climbed gingerly in beside David came flooding back to me; at the same time, I was reminded of a hymn we used to sing at school assembly, "God Moves in a Mysterious Way." The Almighty might well do, but so did David Johnson. The P2 turned out to be his 1934 Rolls-Royce Phantom II which had just been gloriously reupholstered, and the eighteen-year-old he had brought with him, who had passed his driving test only months beforehand, would have to drive either it or the Aston Martin back to Bletchley.

Smashing up a Rolls would have dented even David's considerable bank balance and I was handed the keys of the Aston. I stalled only once and beat my boss back to the office by at least ten minutes without once going over 100 mph (no open road speed limits in those days). I smiled gently to myself as I switched off the engine: yes, I was right to have turned down Associated Octel; burning up petrol was a lot more fun than taking the lead out of it.

David Johnson was, like another bearing that surname, an eccentric fellow; his attitude to work was – how shall I put it? – cavalier. One of his allotted tasks was to educate me in the techniques of valuation. He was a fully qualified member of the Royal Institution of Chartered Surveyors (RICS) and knew precisely how a house valuation should be conducted. But he was not a good teacher. When carrying out building society mortgage valuations, he liked to get things done and dusted as quickly as possible so he could get on with the things that really interested him, like collecting old cars. A valuation meant jumping into his Aston Martin, summoning me to the seat beside him, and whizzing round ten to fifteen properties in a morning, never stopping at one of them.

'Er, David, don't we have to look inside?'

'What for, Charlie? You and I know what it's worth, don't we?'

'Maybe. But I thought –'

'Don't bother. Leave it to me.'

I gather "drive-by" valuations were not unusual at the time, so I'm sure David was not the only surveyor to indulge in this swift but decidedly unprofessional practice. Given his tutelage, you will not be surprised to learn that I never mastered the exams that would have allowed me to call myself Charles Ross RICS. Dentistry – delete. Surveying – delete. Then what? That longcase clock was still ticking.

Two other David Johnson stories stick in my mind. The first concerned his passion for vintage transport and, incongruously, Australian bushfires. His father, ever indulgent towards his only son, had bought him a few thousand acres of rough farmland in Australia. One day, the man who managed David's antipodean estate sent an urgent telegram asking permission to buy a fire appliance to cope with the increasingly serious threat posed by bush fires.

David's eyes lit up. Fire appliance? No need to buy one because he already had precisely what they needed. A vintage Dennis fire engine that he had picked up at auction was duly crated and shipped out to Australia. It is not known how his manager responded (probably in words that I daren't repeat here), nor how much of the estate remained unburned by the time the ancient appliance arrived.

Finally, there is the story of David Johnson and Miss Bletchley – no, not what you're thinking: there was no "me too" in 1970. A bit of background. Though he loved his old vehicles, David did not always keep them in good running order. Maintenance was left to his overworked sixty-year-old manservant/farmhand/gardener/garage mechanic who, like a character out of P.G. Wodehouse, was always referred to simply as "Bass" (like the beer). Bass did his best to keep the cars going, but he was no specialist and wouldn't have lasted more than thirty seconds in the pits at nearby Silverstone.

Whatever failings they may have had under the bonnet, after a bit of polish David's cars looked good, and the organising committee of the annual Miss Bletchley competition asked if he would lend one of his more spectacular vehicles to parade the winner through the thronging streets of their otherwise rather drab town. David was only too pleased to help and generously offered the Phantom II.

When the day came, David drove the Rolls to the podium where the winner was to be chosen and lowered the hood. On came the swim-suited contestants. The crowd cheered, the judges leered, and Miss Bletchley 1970 was chosen. After a few words from the perspiring mayor, the newly crowned winner stepped graciously into the plush leather interior of her car and the parade moved slowly off down the town's main thoroughfare, Queensway, in the summer sunshine.

All was sweetness and light.

Not for long! As the Rolls emerged from the shadow of the railway bridge at the west end of Queensway, it suddenly and inexplicably died. The Phantom had given up the ghost. David jumped down to take a look, while behind him Miss Bletchley, making the most of the moment, carried on waving elegantly to the packed crowds on either side of the street.

'Drat!' muttered David as he emerged from beneath the bonnet. 'We need a tow.' He sprinted into the nearby Johnson office to phone Bass and ask him to bring a second vehicle. On returning, he found Miss Bletchley's waving was flagging a bit. Five minutes later, she shrugged and sat back fanning herself to wait for the relief vehicle. By now, the crowd was also beginning to lose interest. They chatted amongst themselves and looked around for the nearest ice-cream stall.

Bass duly appeared driving another vehicle from David's eclectic collection, a handsome two-tone 1950s MG Magnette. With his boss's help, Bass attached a tow rope between the Rolls and MG, jumped into his car and started the engine. Back in the Phantom, a relieved Miss Bletchley stood up and gallantly resumed her waving. The Magnette was a strong car and if properly serviced could pull a caravan with little difficulty. But David's car had not been well-serviced and the Rolls was not a caravan.

Bass revved the engine and let out the clutch. The tow rope tautened and the Rolls moved forward a foot or two, then stopped. A cloud of blue-black smoke billowed from beneath the MG, engulfing David and his unfortunate passenger. The poor girl began coughing violently and sat down again.

'Fire!' shouted someone in the crowd.

'No!' bellowed Bass through the open window of the MG. 'Bloody clutch has burned out.'

He was right. The Rolls was more tank than caravan and the strain on the MG's clutch was too great. Unable to transfer power to the wheels, the car's engine roared impotently, like a caged lion, leaving tower and towed stranded in the middle of Queensway. A tear – disappointment or smoke? – trickled down Miss Bletchley's face. *Wish I'd never won this sodding competition* was written all over her smoke-smudged face. Understandably.

The day was saved by the wag in the crowd who had shouted 'Fire!' Eager for more attention, and believing he was making a joke, he yelled, "Ere, there's a bloke with a lorry over there. 'E'll do it.'

David didn't see the joke. Rather, he did not believe it was a joke. He went over to the red London Brick Company lorry parked in a side street and chatted to the driver. A note or two changed hands, and before long the lorry had been linked by chain to the front of the MG.

'Brakes off!' shouted the lorry driver.

'Right-o!' chorused David and Bass.

Slowly, very slowly, the extraordinary procession set off down Queensway: an LBC lorry pulling an MG pulling a Rolls-Royce in which Miss Bletchley 1970, tears wiped away and smiling again, was waving bravely to the crowd. She may have smelt more like a kipper than a beauty queen, but she had decided not to let these incompetent men ruin her day. On reaching her destination, the Conservative Club at the east end of Queensway, she even had the good grace to thank David for letting her ride in his car. What a girl! I don't think even I would have been so polite!

I described my employers, W.S. Johnson & Co, as sellers of livestock. If that conjures up an image of me standing with a crook before bleating flocks and lowing herds in a sort of bucolic Bletchley nativity pageant, you'd be only half right. Our staple commodities were indeed cattle and sheep, but I was mainly allowed to cut my auctioneer's teeth (so to speak) on one of our sidelines: chickens.

Much of the auctioning of live animals was done by Dick Arnold, the plain-speaking partner who had told me at interview that I could bugger off if I couldn't sell houses. Fortunately, I did sell a few. More importantly, as far as my future was concerned, I sold a great many chickens and other fowl. Dick had handed me the gavel because he noticed that I had a sharp eye, a quick wit and an easy manner. Watching him flog crates of pullets, pens of Southdown sheep and frisky Friesian bullocks was the only training I ever had.

I didn't find auctioneering difficult. There wasn't much scope for jokes in the Bletchley livestock market – the farmers didn't want any fancy stuff, nor did the Pakistani immigrant workers who bought most of the chickens at between half-a-crown (two shillings and sixpence) and three shillings and ninepence for a pen, each containing four or five live birds. The purchaser was responsible for neck wringing, plucking and gutting. All I had to do was keep my wits about me, speak clearly, and urge bidders up by thruppence (three pennies) at a time. My only difficulty was writing down in English the Urdu names of the successful bidders. This did not apply in the run-up to Christmas when I was promoted from chickens to turkeys – 967 (I can remember the figure exactly) in the week ending at 6 pm on 24 December. Fortunately, turkeys featured only rarely in my future career – none of the cars I have sold at Pebble Beach fall into this category.

By 1971, my career as a surveyor/estate agent was coming along nicely. I had managed, somehow, to pass the first and intermediate RICS exams, and the partners of W.S. Johnson reckoned I was a suitable candidate for a partnership. What I now needed, they declared, was a greater breadth of experience. That involved moving to London for a while to work with one of the leading real estate businesses.

My first interview was with Bertram & Co. It ended with a remark of classic old-world formality: 'And, Mr Ross, if you do come to work with us, you won't be wearing that shirt, will you?'

In city offices, white shirts were "de rigueur, old boy!" ("old boys" were everywhere in those days). The shirt I had bought at great expense especially for the interview was pale blue.

No, I did not work for Bertram's. Instead, I was employed by Richard Ellis, at the time one of the capital's largest and most successful firms of surveyors and valuers. Goodbye crates of chickens and drive-by valuations, hello bowler hats, furled umbrellas and smart offices in Cornhill.

My Richard Ellis year is now a bit of a blur. Though I found the work dull, London certainly perked up my social life. I didn't miss Bletchley, but I did miss the rostrum and the Christmas birds. In their place were valuations of grand properties, including the Café Royal in Regent Street, and dismal industrial premises. On one occasion I was sent to Warrington to value a factory that made custard cream biscuits. I was horrified to find birds flying about inside the building and doing their business into the huge steaming vats of sickly yellow biscuit-filler. I have never eaten a custard cream since.

My most memorable professional experience came on my first day at work. At lunchtime, the junior staff organised a game of basketball, surveyors vs secretaries. I can't remember who won, but I do remember my acute embarrassment when, returning to the office bathrooms to get changed after the match, I couldn't find my trousers.

'Ah, the old trick, Charlie,' explained a man who had been with the company for a year or two.

'What trick?'

'It's the boss's idea of a joke. Every time someone new starts at the office, he hides their trousers in his office while they're out to lunch.'

Fresh up from the country, I believed him and marched off in my underpants to the office of the head of department,

Idris Pearce. Knock, knock.

'Yes?'

'Excuse me, sir, but may I have my trousers back, please?'

'Your what, Ross?'

'My trousers, sir.'

'For goodness' sake, stop wasting my time and get out! I have no idea where your trousers are.'

'I think you do, sir!'

With that, I started rummaging in his desk drawers. Quite why I didn't get the sack there and then, I shall never know. I suppose Pearce had a sense of humour among his many other fine qualities: he went on to become Sir Idris Pearce, President of the RICS. When I eventually returned to my desk with a considerable flea in my ear, I found my neatly folded trousers waiting for me inside an internal mail envelope.

Two episodes from my London social life at the time might be worth mentioning. The first involved a midnight sack race against my brother down Shaftesbury Avenue after a performance of *Rigoletto* at the English National Opera. We sang *La donna è mobile* as we jumped, me more or less in tune, Stewart less so. Fortunately, our voices were muffled by the World War II gas masks we were wearing. Don't ask.

The second episode introduces Alan Downer, another of the W.S. Johnson & Co partners but by no means a typical North Bucks chartered surveyor. Eschewing his colleagues' tweed jackets and brown brogues, he sported a selection of suave double-breasted pin-striped suits, bright silk ties and black slip-on shoes that my mother condemned as "brothel creepers". I doubt that Alan frequented brothels – his wife Rosemary would soon have put a stop to that – but had he done so, he would have glided in, not crept.

Donald Magwitch-Klein, one of Alan's wealthiest and therefore most important clients, was arriving in the UK from

Australia to discuss weighty business. To Alan's irritation, Donald wrote to say he was bringing his teenage daughter, Avril, with him "to see a bit of the Old Country." The last thing Alan wanted was a naïve thirteen-year-old eavesdropping and probably interrupting his business meeting, so he asked me if I'd be a good chap and entertain the girl for the evening. To sweeten the pill, he bought two tickets for the trendy musical *Hair* and handed over a wadge of cash for dinner.

Avril was neither thirteen nor naïve. She turned out to be an extremely sophisticated seventeen-year-old who was longing to see *Hair* – a show I'd never heard of – and was dressed for the part in Cuban heels, rings, beads, flared jeans and a psychedelic top. I turned up looking like a country bumpkin on his night out (which I was) in an ill-fitting suit and yellow kipper tie. Sitting in the stalls watching the hippy cast take their clothes off and the audience cavorting on stage with them, I had never felt so awkward.

Happily, Avril didn't seem to mind my naïvety and we got on quite well. So well, in fact, that at the end of the evening she asked me if I'd escort her back to her hotel, The Dorchester. Was everything going to turn out OK in the end? No, it wasn't. When we reached the foyer and I offered to take her up to her room, she gave me a brotherly kiss on the cheek and said it would be better if she went up alone 'in case we wake up daddy.' She was sharing a suite with her father.

After a year with Richard Ellis, I returned to Buckinghamshire to work for the newly formed Milton Keynes Development Corporation (MKDC). This was all part of the W.S. Johnson planned path to partnership. Had I been interested in planning Milton Keynes or surveying or compulsory purchase or drainage or any of the technicalities associated with the creation of a new city, the job with MKDC would have been a perfect opportunity. Unfortunately, I wasn't interested in any of those things and can't recall a single episode from my year with the Corporation other than my repeated failure to pass the RICS final exams that would have made me a qualified surveyor.

I blame the longcase clock.

My two years of corporate experience completed, I returned to W.S. Johnson & Co. Not the Bletchley office this time but a recently acquired branch in the former county town of Buckingham. The office was in a four-storey 18th-century building in Market Square. When David Johnson discovered that the original half-timbered façade had been rendered over – and not being one to follow what he considered petty rules (remember the drive-by valuations?) – he had the rendering removed without consulting the local planning authorities. Bad move. The building was Grade II listed, which meant any alteration required official consent, and the irked planner ordered David to replace the rendering at considerable cost. No new cars for him that year.

The Buckingham office was managed by a man who had more influence on my career than anyone else. It is almost certainly true that had I not worked with John Collings, I would not be where I am today. This book is, in a way, a tribute to his influence.

John was a short, wiry yet immensely strong Welshman who drifted into Buckingham in the 1950s and remained there for the rest of his life. He had known nothing about the place but came, he said, because he liked the sound of it. The town took to him immediately and he was given a job with Osbornes, one of the local estate agents. When I tell you that Mr Osborne, like John, was also an auctioneer and his office had a saleroom, you can probably guess where this story is going.

On retirement, Osborne sold his business to John, who

built it up and then sold it to W.S. Johnson and Co. Enter Charlie Ross, fresh from the corporate world of Richard Ellis and the MKDC, to work in the Buckingham branch alongside John Collings. I felt like Tigger in the Winnie-the-Pooh story where he discovers what he *really* likes for breakfast. John and I were quite good at selling houses, and he was kind enough to let me have the commission on some that he had sold. But what we both really liked, what kept us chatting for hours, what made coming in to work each morning a true pleasure, were the objects that passed through the saleroom.

On the surface, we didn't have a great deal in common. I was a well-built Englishman, he a lean Welshman; I had spent my early manhood chasing girls around London; he had spent his in prisoner-of-war camps where he and his colleagues had held to attention the frozen corpse of a colleague so as to get his bread ration. But we shared an interest in cars – his was a two-seater Volvo P1800 like that driven by Simon Templar in *The Saint* – and an enthusiasm for old and beautiful things. We both thoroughly enjoyed auctioneering.

John learned about antique clocks and musical boxes, his passion, by taking them to pieces, bit by intricate bit, repairing and reassembling them in perfect working order. I was no restorer or repairer, but I learned about furniture, silver, paintings and other antiques because I appreciated their workmanship – and because I needed to know about them in order to sell them. So began my *real* education.

CHAPTER FOUR

Starting with Spraggs

John Collings was the best auctioneer I have had the pleasure to witness. He was an actor, his stage the former grain store that served as W.S. Johnson & Co's Morton Road auction saleroom. It was certainly no Christie's. From the street, it looked like a disused garage; inside, it resembled the props room of a provincial theatre. Smelling of furniture polish, old barley and cigar smoke, it was piled to its nicotine-stained ceiling with faded watercolours, an elephant's foot wastepaper basket, silver-plated cruets, a tapestry-seated commode, dozens of Victorian balloon back chairs, a vintage lawnmower, and a couple of gloomy Victorian dressers that were too large for any modern home. Here, in this splendid hugger-mugger of former glories, John held court.

Standing on the rostrum, his silver-grey hair and moustache highlighted against the dirty window behind him, John was not an imposing figure. But when he opened his mouth to speak, both he and the room around him were transformed. No Gielgud or Guinness could have held an audience so completely, and I am convinced that had he joined the RSC instead of W.S. Johnson & Co, he would have made a memorable Hamlet. Sadly, yet fortunately for me, the nearest he came to the immortal Dane was the name on the packet of small cigars he smoked incessantly.

Day after day, week after week, I watched and learned as he flattered and joked his way into his audience's hearts, always with a gracious manner, a winning smile and a twinkle in the eye. John's affection for his fellow human beings was all the more remarkable considering the harrowing experiences as a POW that I alluded to in the previous chapter.

'Mr Plimsoll!' he would exclaim in his sing-song Welsh voice when spotting a former punter putting in a bid. 'A pleasure to see you here again. You're in for five pounds ten? Well done, sir!'

While to another, 'Oh, come along madam! I seem to remember you paid twice as much for the picture you bought last month, and this one's of even better quality. Please don't let me down!'

Or, 'Surely you don't want to be beaten by a gentleman, Miss Wilkins? Another five bob – for the sake of the Pankhursts!'

John taught me much more than the art of auctioneering. Before working with him, I liked antiques but knew precious little about them. Though I understood that a stool was not necessarily what the doctors had examined when I was suspected of having had polio, I knew Sheraton as either a hotel or a mispronounced 18th-century playwright. John set me straight. Unlike most of those who had attempted to fill my head with facts at school, his method was direct, crude even, but unfailingly memorable.

'How old is that cruet, John?'

'Made at about the same time as Queen Mary's knickers,

Charlie. But better quality.'

'Er, John, how can you be so sure those chairs are Victorian?'

'Because our friend George Chippendale wouldn't have made anything so hideous, even with one hand behind his back and his eyes closed.'

'Those silver candlesticks for next week's sale, John, why haven't they got a lion stamped on them?'

'There's no lion on them, Charlie my boy, because they're not bloody silver.'

'But they look like silver.'

'Of course they do. Look posh but aren't, like my Auntie Annie in the cat fur coat she picked up at the pawnbroker in Penarth. They're silver plate, Charlie. Only the real thing – solid right through – has a lion on it.'

John taught me the way he himself had been taught, keeping eyes and ears open and picking things up as one goes along. He launched his career as an estate agent and auctioneer when he returned home to Wales after the war. His employers clearly thought highly of him, otherwise – as he explained to me one afternoon – he would have lost his job before he had hardly started.

His boss, who had an eye for a bargain, had been instructed by the Ministry of Defence to sell a large quantity of armed forces furniture that was surplus to requirements after the end of World War II. All the items were well made. Following the delivery of dozens of chests of drawers, tables and wardrobes, John and a young colleague were given the task of "lotting them up", ie chalking a lot number on each piece. It was tedious work. Having numbered most of the pieces by their lunch hour, John and his friend went down to the pub for a sandwich and a beer or two.

Or two? When they returned, three or four pints later, they blinked at the remaining rows of wardrobes standing like sentry boxes of recent memory, picked up their sticks of chalk, and finished the lotting up. Over the next five days, prospective buyers inspected the furniture and jotted down the lot numbers of articles they wished to bid for. So far, so good.

On the Saturday of the auction, the saleroom was crammed and the auction, which lasted several hours, went far better than expected. After the last lot was sold, the successful bidders came forward to pay for and collect their acquisitions. That's when the fun started.

'Lot number 267, sir? That's the wardrobe over there.'

Irate businessman pushes forward. 'Excuse me, but I bought that wardrobe. Lot number 336.'

'I'm sorry sir, but that wardrobe is Lot number 267.'

'No it's not! Are you calling me a liar? Come over here and take a look for yourself. 336, as plain as a pikestaff.'

He was right. In fact both purchasers were right. Returning half cut from the pub and forgetting which wardrobes he had already lotted up, John had put a second lot number on the back of those he had marked in the morning. Each wardrobe, therefore, bore two numbers and had been sold twice over. No wonder the auction had gone better than expected.

John never explained how his boss sorted things out. In the end, however, he saw the amusing side of the debacle and John was not sacked. But it was, he said, parodying the Duke of Wellington, a 'close-run thing'.

I had been working with John for a month or two when I had a close-run thing of my own. One sunny Wednesday morning in May, John stopped halfway through an auction, smiled at the audience and announced, as if it were the most normal thing in the world, 'Well, thank you everyone. Mr Ross will now take over.'

I have already alluded to the most precious gift my father

left me. It was not the broken Timex watch, nor the pair of worn Spanish trainers, nor the defunct hearing aid, all of which the hospital where he had died handed over to Stewart and me in a plastic bag. No, the bequest for which I remain truly grateful was his ability to think quickly.

As John stepped down from the rostrum and handed me the gavel, my genetic inheritance took control. Pointing to a silver toast rack, off I went. My career as a bona fide auctioneer of antiques was launched.

It very nearly sank the moment it hit the water.

At this point, I need to remind those not familiar with auctions of two things. First, when the hammer comes down, that's it. End of story. No more bids. Item sold. Second, many people entering an item in an auction do so with a "reserve", a minimum price they are prepared to accept. If that price is not reached, the piece is returned to the owner or held over for a future auction.

Bearing these two things in mind, I begin.

'Where would you like to start?' I ask, glancing as confidently as I could at the sea of faces before me. 'Five pounds anyone?'

Not a flutter.

'Three pounds then?'

A man with a Players Embassy hanging from his bottom lip waves the sale catalogue to show he's in.

'Thank you, sir. Three pounds ten shillings [£3.50], someone?'

Yes, a silver-haired lady with scarlet lipstick lifts a many-ringed finger.

Onward and upward we go. *This is a piece of cake*, I say to myself. *Fun, too.* Behind me, John Collings watches in silence.

I finally bring the hammer down at £6.00. I turn to the purchaser, a corpulent fellow in tweeds with a large handlebar moustache and a pork pie hat. He reminds me of the self-important, old-school types that were being mocked every week in *Monty Python's Flying Circus*.

'Name, sir?' I ask politely.

'Spraggs,' he barks, adding unnecessarily, 'Major!'

I'm right, I think. Straight out of *Monty Python*. I look down at my sale sheet. There it is in black and white, "Toast rack, hallmarked silver, Birmingham, 1935." I run my eye further across the page to the figures in red ink in the "Reserve" column.

What the … ? Crikey! It has a reserve of £12. Now it's sold, that's the sum (less commission) we have to give the former owner. The pompous Spraggs will pay £6.00 and the remainder will have to come out of my wages. I'm on £3.00 a week.

Behind me, John Collings moves not a muscle. 'Thought I'd let you learn on the job, Charlie,' he chuckled afterwards.

The thought of staying away from The Swan and Castle for a fortnight demanded desperate measures.

'Mr Spraggs?'

'Major!'

'Oh yes! I do apologise. Major Spraggs, I'm terribly sorry, but there's been a small mistake.'

'Eh? What?'

'You're in at six pounds, sir, but –' I stare intently at the wall at the back of the room '– I have a bid of seven.'

Still no movement behind me.

The Major heaves himself around and glares at the wall. There is no one there, certainly no one bidding. I have fallen back on an old auctioneer's technique that I had seen John employ. It's known as taking a bid "off the chandelier" in order to meet the reserve.

'Eight!' harrumphs the Major.

I cap it with £8-10-0 (£8.50) from the back of the room. Back and forth we go, wall–Major–wall–Major, until the wall drops out at the required £12.00 and I bring the hammer down a second time. Spraggs finally has his silver toast rack.

'Don't you ever do that again,' comes a voice from behind me.

'I won't, John. Promise,' I reply.

And I haven't. Though my wages have now risen above £3.00 a week, the idea of selling a Ferrari for $4.6 million when it has a reserve of $7 million does not bear thinking about.

Not all errors have unfortunate consequences. Early on in my Buckingham years, we received a phone call from a woman who asked us to clear her garden shed of 'bits of broken old furniture'.

I hesitated. We did not run a rubbish removal service.

'Do you think any of it will fetch much at auction?' I asked tactfully.

'Not a clue but shouldn't think so. Fifty pounds or so at the most. It'd be a shame to burn it, but my husband wants somewhere dry to keep his old lawnmower.'

I made an appointment and went round to the woman's house to check the contents of the shed. She was right. Most of the stuff in there was rubbish, but perhaps a buyer could be found for the dilapidated walnut bureau tucked away in a cobwebby corner. With no back, feet or handles, it was just a hulk, like those left rotting on the edge of Portsmouth harbour. Nevertheless, John had taught me about the growing interest in what were known in the trade as "untouched" (ie falling to bits) items suitable for expert restoration, and I put a reserve on it of £100 – a great deal of money in the early 1970s. While the woman was delighted, I hoped I had not made a dreadful mistake.

I hadn't.

Two weeks later, I received a second call from the woman, now known in the office as "Mrs Bureau".

'Mr Ross?'

'Speaking. How can I help?'

'I think you've made a serious mistake,' she explained angrily.

'I hope not, madam. Has something gone wrong?'

'Yes, it has. You've sent me someone else's cheque.'

I smiled and mouthed 'Mrs Bureau' to John, who was standing beside me.

'I think you have received the right cheque, madam. One thousand, one hundred and sixty pounds?'

There was a long silence, followed by a penitent, 'Yes, that's it. I'm sorry I was a bit cross just now, but I don't understand.'

'The bureau, madam. The other items were, as you suggested, worthless. But it was not. Perhaps a new lawnmower for your husband and even a new shed for him to keep it in?'

Over the years, I have learned when little jokes like that are acceptable and when they are not. It's a matter of tact and sensitivity, remembering that the customer is always right (except in the case of Major Spraggs). This rule was not followed by Michael Mounsey, the dour, academic public schoolmaster who handled our auctions when neither John nor I were available. He was strong on detail and very helpful when drawing up a sale catalogue but the kiss of death on the rostrum.

Michael's very presence was lugubrious. Always dressed in a thick woollen cardigan buttoned up to the neck and peering disdainfully at the punters over the top of his half-moon glasses, he resembled an elongated human owl. While John and I prided ourselves on being able to handle one hundred lots in an hour, Michael never went above forty. Nor did he refrain from making his tastes known to the audience. This did not go down well.

In the 1970s, it was fashionable to reupholster old furniture with Dralon. Michael did not approve. One day, returning to the saleroom and asking the staff how the recent Mounsey-managed sale had gone, we were met with eyes rolled in despair. He had auctioned – slowly and with meticulous care – a Victorian nursery chair upholstered in purple Dralon. He brought the gavel down at £15, looked up at the purchaser, a smart middle-aged woman sitting in the centre of the room, and exclaimed, 'Madam, what extraordinary taste you have!'

Thereafter, Michael's services were limited to helping with catalogues. He worked alongside Bert Robinson, the Dickensian clerk who wore the same black double-breasted suit whatever the weather, autumn, winter, spring and summer. His principal task was to write out customer bills. He did this by hand, sometimes three or four hundred in a single day, using a fountain pen. They were never smudged or blotted, probably because the ink dried immediately under the sprinkling of ash that fell continuously from the untipped cigarette glued to his bottom lip.

The woman who bought the Dralon-covered chair reminds me of another of our posher customers. This one was young, attractive, wealthy – and charmingly eccentric. I remember her turning up at one of our sales and joining in the proceedings as if they were a competitive sport, like tennis, that she was determined to win. Whatever the object, she had to have it. Bid followed bid, all cheerfully delivered in her clear BBC voice until, when it was all over, she found to her surprise that she had bought over half the lots. She paid for them without hesitation. However, as the reality of what she had done dawned on her, she asked if we would be good enough to store them for her. We agreed – for a small weekly fee. Three months later, she swept into the office and instructed us to sell everything she had bought. Her loss was considerable, but she didn't seem to mind.

'More money than sense,' muttered John following her departure. I had to agree, though the customer is always right, of course.

John and I made sure the Buckingham saleroom was a fun place to work. Bureaucracy was kept to a minimum and the staff treated as members of a large family. I don't recall any of them leaving to work elsewhere.

The lynchpin of the whole operation was Liz Zettl, our cheerful, multi-talented secretary who would acquire national celebrity as, aged 101, she became the oldest ever court witness in a murder trial. Her posthumous fame rose still higher when she was played by Sheila Hancock in the BBC drama *The Sixth Commandment* (2023) about the trial of Benjamin Field and Martyn Smyth for the murder of Peter Farquhar. My own memories of Liz are less dramatic, though two are worth recording. The first is centred on my thighs.

For genetic reasons I have never understood – there must have been a Victorian strongman somewhere in the family, though no record of him exists – as a young man I sported exceptionally large and powerful thighs. These enabled me to run fast on the wing in rugby and win the long jump competition on school sports day (same distance as Mary Rand's gold medal winning leap in the 1964 Olympics), but they were a serious handicap when it came to buying trousers. Those that fitted round the waist gave the impression of my being poured in hot around the loins; those that fitted around the loins required belting my waist like a concertina. I opted for the former.

In general, my tight trousers took the strain well. However, as I was prancing around the office one day in celebration of a successful sale, they split in two, back to front, down the main seam. Liz looked up from her typewriter and smiled.

'Right, Charlie. Whip them off and I'll sew them up in the back room.' I did as she instructed and sat down at my desk in my underpants.

As luck would have it, a woman came in and asked to see the sales brochure of a house we had for sale in Moreton Road. We had a stock of these brochures in a cupboard on the other side of the room.

'I'm very sorry, madam, but we have run out of brochures. More are being printed, so if you'd like to come back tomorrow –'

'I won't be here tomorrow. How can you have a house for sale in the window but no brochures?'

I silently cursed Marks & Spencer for their weak-seamed trousers. I had three options: (a) try to explain, (b) walk across the room in my pants as if nothing was amiss, (c) call for help. I chose C.

'Liz,' I called over my shoulder, 'a lady here wants to know whether we've got any brochures left for the house in Moreton Road. Are there any back there?'

No reply. Liz could hear me perfectly well but was enjoying the situation too much to spoil it by coming to my rescue.

'Liz!' I called again, louder this time. Still no response.

The woman had had enough. Without another word, she turned and walked out of the office. Still chuckling, Liz returned with my trousers a couple of minutes later. The brochure woman did not buy the house in Moreton Road, not did we see her in the office again.

One more Liz Zettl story, this time with the embarrassment reversed. She was a fine, rapid typist so I was surprised when random spaces started appearing between words and letters in the correspondence she typed. For example: De ar Si r, T hank you fo r yo ur ...

Liz checked her machine and, unable to find anything

wrong with it, called in an Olivetti engineer to take a look. He too could find nothing wrong. A fan of the Sherlock Holmes school of deduction, he suspected that the fault was with the typist rather than with the machine. He asked Liz to type a letter while he stood behind her. The random spaces continued to appear.

The Sherlock of North Buckinghamshire took me to one side and asked if he might have a 'quiet word'. My secretary, he pointed out, was what he called 'a well-proportioned lady', and every now and again her ample bosom inadvertently struck the space bar beneath it. I knew Liz well enough to explain the problem without causing offence. She roared with laughter, moved her chair back a couple of inches, and the mystery of the random spaces was solved.

The highlight of my Buckingham years was personal. Liz made an appointment for me to show my friends Andrew and Ginny Box around Finmere House, a large property whose alcoholic owner had been forced to put it up for sale. The Boxes had a lodger staying with them, a lively young teacher named Sally who had recently started work at nearby Akeley Wood School. As she would have to move to Finmere House with them if they bought it, she tagged along to see what the place was like.

The potential buyers wandered off to look around the house. A good estate agent would have gone with them, explaining why this property was exactly what they were looking for, etc, etc. I chose instead to remain in the hall, chatting – and rapidly falling in love with – the pretty lodger in blue denim dungarees and a bright headscarf. We got on incredibly well. Shortly after our first meeting, she moved into the cottage in Akeley Wood that I had bought with my brother. We were engaged six weeks later and married the following year. Now a loving mother to our two children, Charlotte and Olly, and granny to the four grandchildren,

Finn, Max, Ana and Zac, she remains my best friend and companion. In recent years Sally has become a workmate, too, travelling with me to the US and taking the telephone bids at the Gooding & Company car auctions.

When Sally took me home to meet her parents for the first time, I overheard her mother saying with her customary frankness, 'One of your better efforts, dear.' Flattering, I suppose, though I did wonder what I was being compared with!

By the time of my marriage in 1977, I had begun to pick up extra work as a freelance auctioneer. Emboldened by this, I decided to take the plunge. I handed in my notice to W.S. Johnson & Co, bade a grateful farewell to John Collings, Liz Zettl and the others in the Buckingham office, and struck out on my own. My mother, haunted by what had happened when my father went down this path, was horrified.

CHAPTER FIVE

Bread and Butter

'Don't forget your bread and butter, Charlie,' John Collings called as I walked out of the Morton Road saleroom for the final time. Anyone who has been self-employed will understand that he was not talking about my packed lunch. The boon of an independent worker's life is a source of reliable income. For an actor this used to be TV advert repeat fees; for my brother, a writer, it was children's nonfiction in pre-internet days; for me it was the Finchley auction on Mondays and the High Wycombe one every Saturday. The latter, at fifty quid a throw, was my bread. Finchley, which might earn me twice as much, was the butter. Anything on top of these two gigs was jam.

The High Wycombe sale was the only regular auction I have taken on primarily for the money it brought in. It was not that the people I met there were unpleasant or that the saleroom was particularly shabby; no, it was because the goods I was asked to sell were dull and mind-bogglingly repetitive. Whenever possible, I like to liven up an auction with a little snippet or quip. However, as one MOD surplus desk is much like any other MOD surplus desk, and at High Wycombe I was asked to sell 150 of them in a single afternoon, I had my work cut out.

'Lot number 1 ... is a handsome example of Army carpentry, may well be the very desk that General Montgomery sat at when planning D-Day.'

'Lot number 25 ... is perhaps the desk Kenneth More sat behind while filming *Sink the Bismarck*.'

'Lot number 64 ... is the type of desk before which Spike Milligan may have been hauled for being cheeky to an officer in 1944.'

'Lot number 93 ... is the type of MOD surplus desk with which you are now rather familiar.'

'Lot number 139 ... needs no introduction.'

By the end of the sale I was itching to go home for a much-needed gin and tonic. On the way, I used to think about the size and weight of lots I had been selling and how the porters had struggled to get them out of the saleroom and into waiting lorries and vans. Why did the military feel it necessary to make even their furniture bullet-proof? No wonder the world's running out of forests!

There were moments, too, when on the drive home I pondered my decision to join the ranks of self-employed auctioneers. Recently married and with our first child, Charlotte, on the way, it had been a bit of a gamble. A freelance auctioneer, even more than an actor, is wholly dependent on their voice; if that goes, they go. They cannot afford a bad performance, either. A TV or film actor can have a second take. But there are no second takes on the rostrum: a mishandled bid may cost the buyer or seller ten ... one hundred ... one thousand ... one million pounds. It doesn't bear thinking about – so I don't. I just get on with it, relying on instinct and loving every minute (as long as there are not too many lots of MOD surplus).

North-West London Auctions (now NL Auction Rooms) in Lodge House, Finchley, was quite special. I handled their sales once a week, including bank holidays, Boxing Day and New Year's Day, for twenty years. The typical punter, whether dealer or keen amateur, knew their stuff, and I got to know some of them well. Among such an astute crowd there was no place for army surplus. Instead, we had an array of interesting furniture (much of it antique), porcelain, artwork and silver. Talking of silver, I recall one of the more unusual lots I was called upon to sell – and one of my riskier off-the-cuff comments.

It was May 1979. The days were lengthening and the drive to Finchley between blossoming hedgerows lit by the late afternoon sunshine had been a pleasure. I was in a good mood. The sale went well, too, even the gilt-framed Victorian watercolours fetching well over their reserve prices. As my fee was a percentage of the total value of all lots sold, my spirits rose higher with each successful cry of 'Sold!'

The silver – candlesticks, cruets, cutlery, dishes and other lion-marked items – was placed in the second half of the sale. All were quality but, in auction terms, commonplace. Except for Lot 103.

'And our final piece of silver is rather special. Lot number 103, an antique circumcision set, is definitely a collector's item. Who will start us off? Am I bid fifty pounds? Sixty? Seventy? Yes, thank you, madam. Anyone in for one hundred pounds?' So off we went.

I always do my homework before a sale, going through the catalogue, familiarizing myself with pronunciation, provenance and prices, and making prompt notes on things to refer to or avoid during the auction. Next to Lot 103 I had written "no jokes" and underlined it heavily. I'm not sure whether I didn't see it or deliberately ignored it, but I found the temptation too strong to resist.

'Good afternoon everyone. The bidding stands at six hundred and fifty pounds. Seven hundred anyone? No, then for the first time, a silver antique circumcision set at six hundred and fifty ... for the second time ... and for the third time, at six hundred and fifty ... Sold! Congratulations, sir. A bargain or, if I may say so, a snip.'

Oh my God! What have I just said? And in this part of London, too! For a split second, I felt my presence at this auction, if not my entire career, hung in the balance. I need not have worried. A ripple of appreciative laughter ran around the saleroom and I moved swiftly on to Lot 104. Phew!

My other memory of a Finchley auction concerns an incident that took place when I was on holiday. In my absence, the sale was conducted by a competent but young and inexperienced auctioneer. To save his embarrassment, let's call him Darren. As explained briefly in Chapter Four, clients offering an object for auction often put a reserve price on it – ie a price below which they do not want it sold. During the sale, the auctioneer is permitted to accept an "invisible" bid on behalf of the vendor in an effort to reach the reserve. Such bids, however, may never – and the rules are extremely strict on this – exceed the reserve.

With Darren on the gavel, the sale started well and rolled along merrily until it reached Lot 410, a very ordinary three-piece suite. Darren glanced down at his sale sheet: "Reserve £500". *You'll be lucky to get a quarter of that!* he thought. Nevertheless, duty bound to help a vendor whenever possible, he started the bidding at £100. To his surprise, a young couple at the back of the room immediately came in. *OK*, thought Darren, *let's see if you're serious*. He put in a bid of £150 on behalf of the vendor. The couple at the back responded with £200.

And so it went on until the couple at the back dropped

out at £450. Darren brought the hammer down, unfortunately omitting to say "not sold" and moved on to the next lot. The thwarted young couple walked out in a huff. At the same time, an elderly couple in the front row were nudging themselves and grinning like monkeys. At the end of the sale, as Darren was tidying up his paperwork and preparing to go home, they approached him and shook him warmly by the hand.

'We want to thank you for the wonderful job you did with the three-piece suite,' exclaimed the man.

'Beyond our wildest dreams!' added his wife with a smile as wide as the unsold sofa.

Darren was perplexed. Customers were not usually this excited when the bidding fails to reach their reserve. 'I apologise,' he said. 'I did my best, but surely the reserve of five hundred pounds was a bit optimistic?'

The man looked blank. 'Five hundred pounds? What do you mean? We put a reserve of fifty pounds on it.'

Darren showed them his notes. There it was in the black ink of the auction clerk: "Reserve of £500."

The woman put on her glasses and examined the sheet herself. 'But it doesn't say five hundred pounds, Mr, er …'

'Wilkins. Darren Wilkins.'

'Well, Mr Wilkins, I think you will find that the last nought is not a nought but a "D".'

'Eh?' Darren looked at the figure again.

The woman was right. The clerk had written "Reserve £50D", meaning a reserve price of £50 and leaving the auctioneer at their D[iscretion] to accept a lower bid if the bidding stalls before the reserve. The misreading was an easy mistake to make, though a costly one. The young couple had lost out on the suite of their dreams while the elderly pair were bitterly disappointed to be left with three bits of furniture they thought had finally sold at an exceptionally competitive price. Darren should, of course, have said "not sold".

The following week, Charlie Ross had returned from holiday and conducted the Finchley auction himself. The managers were relieved to see that he went through his sheet very carefully with the clerk before starting the sale.

Around this time I began doing charity auctions. I love these shows, for that is what most of them are, pure theatre. The audience is there to be generous in support of a worthy cause and to have fun, often assisted by plenty of fine food and drink, and it's my job to make sure neither they nor the charity are disappointed. The occasional joke goes down well.

To a man looking anxiously around him, 'Go on sir! It costs you nothing to bid!'

And to someone who thinks they've got a bargain, 'Stop smiling, madam – I haven't brought the hammer down yet!'

I would eventually graduate to million-pound charity auctions attended by the great and (usually) good in spectacular venues all around the world. In my thirties, however, I was cutting my teeth at a series of very jolly but by no means glamorous events. I was going to say that this is how I learned my trade as a charity auctioneer; in fact, one never stops learning. No two audiences are the same. A remark that brings roars of laughter on a Friday is met with an uncomprehending silence on Saturday. Tastes and fashions change, too. Some of the banter from my early days – like that of many performers back then – might well get me into hot water today. Probably quite correctly.

An example of how things have changed comes from one of my first charity auctions. Before the birth of our first child, Sally attended classes run by the Natural Childbirth Trust (NCT). A few months later, her friend Fiona Godfrey suggested it would be a good idea to hold an auction to raise money for this very worthwhile charity. Friends and acquaintances were asked to donate saleable items and I was invited to conduct the auction. People's idea of what a "saleable item" is varies considerably. The catalogue for this auction included:

> bottles of booze, ranging from fine malt whisky to out-of-date Lambrusco
>
> home-make cakes in a variety of sizes and types
>
> a chauffeur-driven car to and from a London airport
>
> pots of jam and marmalade (numerous, all sizes)
>
> four alloy wheels for a Ford Cortina (pre-owned??)

No matter how passionate the audience was about the NCT, and no matter how persuasive my auctioneering, it was going to be a tough sell. When I mentioned this to Peter, the husband of Sally's friend Fiona who was organising the event, he grinned and disappeared into a room he called his study. He emerged a few moments later carrying a large bundle of magazines.

'Here you are, Charlie,' he said, handing them over. 'Add one or two of these to a lot that's struggling and I'm sure it'll perk up.'

I groan inwardly. I honestly didn't think that a couple of copies of *Country Life* would do much to enhance the market appeal of lemon drizzle. I thank him and glance down at the front covers. Well, this is certainly not country life as experienced in North Bucks: the magazines are *Playboy*!

To my further surprise, the wheeze works.

'Come along, everyone, surely a pot of delicious home-made marmalade is worth more than two pounds fifty? No? I'll tell you what, I'll spice the lot up, titivate it you might say, by throwing in the March and April editions of … *Playboy*!'

I show the centrefolds to the grinning audience. This is more like it.

'As you can see, the lot now comprises a jar of marmalade and a couple of Playmates. Any advance on two pounds fifty?'

'Three pounds!'

'Thank you, madam. What about three fifty?'

Six pairs of hands wave eagerly. The lot eventually goes for fifteen quid – to the vicar!

Two or three auctions a week were sufficient to keep the wolf from the door, but not to stop him sniffing around the windows. To persuade the beast to clear off altogether, a little bit of extra cash was needed. Return to estate agency? Been there, got the t-shirt, and had no wish to return. Admit defeat, swot, and re-sit my A-Levels alongside serried ranks of teenagers in a smelly sports hall? Thank you, but no. So where was the missing bonus to come from?

The answer appeared to lie under my very nose. At Finchley and High Wycombe a fair proportion of the lots I sold were bought by dealers, smart characters who spotted a bargain and re-sold it (perhaps after applying a little Kiwi boot polish to the faded woodwork) at a tidy profit. Money for old rope, yes?

No.

I was not, am not, and never will be a natural dealer. As evidence I present the solid but unspectacular brown wooden bookcase that sits against the wall in our sitting room. Its contents – books on antiques, some of my brother's many volumes, and a handsome collection of *Wisden Cricketers' Almanack* dating back (in facsimile) to 1879 – are camouflage, my attempt to hide the look on its mahogany face. Whenever I glance towards it, the shelves spread themselves into a mocking grin. It doesn't speak because it doesn't need to. The look says it all: *Call yourself a dealer, Charlie? You couldn't even deal a pack of cards!*

The evidence? Well, long ago, when petrol cost about

£1.00 a *gallon*, I bought this bookcase for a cool £2,000. Today, when petrol is about £1.50 a *litre*, I'd be lucky to get £300. No, I am not one of the world's great dealers. QED.

When buying, you see, I don't have much of an eye for a bargain. To make things harder, I am also not particularly good at auctions. I shall rephrase that. I might be quite good at *selling* things at auction, but I am pretty useless at *buying* them. This is well borne out in a two-act tragicomedy that I would entitle *A Comedy of Errors* if someone hadn't thought up the title before me.

Act I: John Deeley meets William IV, eventually

John Deeley was a farmer, neighbour and friend who came into a bit of money by selling off farmland for the construction of the M40 motorway. Now they had the means to do so, he and his wife Linda began to collect antiques. John was a careful man and rather than splurge on overpriced furniture from an antique shop in, say, Oxford or Woodstock, he liked to attend local sales on the lookout for quality pieces at sensible prices. The announcement of a two-day sale of the contents of a semi-stately home aroused his interest and he went along to one of the view days to see what was on offer.

Ah-ha! Yes, just what he had been looking for: a charming rosewood table. But what was it worth and, if it looked as if it might go for a reasonable price, who could he ask to help him with the bidding process? The answer came to him in a flash.

'Charlie, John here. What do you know about tables?'

'A bit. Why?'

He explained, and I agreed to help. The following day, we inspected the piece he was interested in. It was a William IV rosewood centre table worth, in my estimation, something in the region of £300. As the sale was in Stratton Audley, a village only three or so miles from where I lived, I also agreed to accompany him and bid on his behalf. I knew the auctioneers, too, and assured him that I understood how these things worked.

The day came and I stationed myself beside John as our lot came up. The bidding started at £100 and climbed slowly. I nudged John.

'Looks like we're in luck,' I whispered. He nodded and gave me a thumbs up.

As the bidding crawled over £200, I held fire. The best time to jump in, I knew from experience, was when the other punters were losing their nerve.

'I have two hundred and sixty pounds,' announced the auctioneer. 'Anyone prepared to go to two hundred and eighty?'

When I raised my hand, the auctioneer gave me a knowing if somewhat surprised look.

'Ah, thank you, sir. I have a bid on my left of two hundred and eighty pounds. Do I have three hundred?' Not a flicker. 'Very well then, for the first time at two hundred and eighty pounds ... second time ... third time ... Sold!'

I gave John a self-satisfied grin and said quietly, so as not to draw attention to myself, 'Well done, John. I am surprised –' when I was interrupted by the auctioneer.

'And now Lot number 267, the William IV rosewood centre table.'

It was my turn to interrupt. 'I beg your pardon,' I called out, not caring whether I drew attention to myself or not, 'but I've just bought that lot.'

'I'm sorry sir, but you have not. You bought Lot number 266.'

I couldn't believe it! Such an elementary error occurred only when dealers failed to check their lot numbers carefully. Memories of imperfectly done homework with doodles of cricket shots in the margin flashed before my glazed eyes.

Humiliated, I muttered, 'Well, what have I bought?'

The auctioneer grinned and confided softly, 'A 1930s upright piano,' adding, 'sir' to rub in the humiliation. Fortunately, we knew each other well enough to have a laugh about it a couple of weeks afterwards. But not at the time.

I was floundering. 'Er, can't you put it up again?'

'I'm afraid not. Now, sir, with your permission, I will resume the auction.' Raising his voice, he announced with scarcely concealed amusement, 'Lot number 267, the rosewood table – shall we start at one hundred and fifty pounds …?'

To help John Deeley and save a little face, I did bid successfully for the William IV table, securing it for £310. I finally managed to dispose of the out-of-tune and virtually unplayable piano for £50 three weeks later.

Moral of the story? By all means ask Charlie Ross to sell an item for you – but take care before asking him to buy something on your behalf. He's an auctioneer, you see, not a dealer. If you don't believe me, see what other blunder he made at the very same sale.

Act II : Look Before you Strike

To my intense embarrassment, I made a second howler at the very same sale. This time I was acting for myself, wearing my dealer's hat. During the preview, I had made a list of all the pieces I thought might earn me a few quid if I could get them at a decent price. The back of my envelope contained a nursing chair, a Georgian card table, a pair of silver candlesticks c.1800, and a 19th-century longcase clock that reminded me of the one that had stood in the corridor of Uncle Mac's practice in Cavendish Square. With a mahogany case and, judging by the dials and key holes on the face, an eight-day mechanism, I estimated it to be worth somewhere between £400 and £500.

A dealer buying antiques for a client in the Netherlands bought the nursing chair for what I regarded as a silly price, and the card table proved out of my league; I almost bought the candlesticks but pulled out when I remembered that my car would need a couple of front tyres before its MOT the following week. That left Lot 306, the eight-day longcase – ie "grandfather" – clock.

The bidding opened at £100, and I joined in. Imagine my delight when, after two further bids, I found myself the only one still in. My final bid of £150 was accepted and the gavel came down to bring the sale to a close. I had been so engrossed by my bargain that I had taken no notice of what was going on around me. Had I done so, I would have seen the dealers in the crowd laughing quietly to themselves.

The laugh's on me, chaps! I thought as I made my way over to my new acquisition in order to examine the precision movement that gave these clocks their deep, distinctive tick-tock sound. With the sale attendant's permission, I slid the hood forward and peered inside at the finely crafted cogs and springs of brass and steel, and the long chains bearing the grey lead weights that powered the whole mechanism ...

Except there were no finely crafted cogs, brass or otherwise; nor any steel springs; and the clock was powered not by lead weights but by a pair of size A Eveready batteries. The original clockwork had been stripped out and replaced by the sort of electric mechanism found in nearly all modern clocks. It was probably worth about half what I had paid for it.

I had not been swindled; I had simply failed to do what any decent dealer would do: thoroughly check an item before bidding for it. I loaded the Eveready grandfather clock into the car, took it home and stuck it in the garage. There it stayed until its batteries ran flat.

CHAPTER SIX

Plimsolls

I suggested a couple of chapters earlier that if I had any training for the podium, it was in the theatre. Fun, action theatre. Shakespeare was OK as long as it was *The Merry Wives of Windsor*, with lots of pranks and rushing about. I don't think I would have got on too well with one of the Bard's more cerebral plays with their long ponderings on love, ambition, indecision and so forth. Many years ago, someone (probably Stewart) took me to see a performance of *Waiting for Godot*. I fell asleep after about half an hour and still don't know whether he turned up.

Film was a big early influence, too. My favourite actor was Kenneth More, and some of the great British movies of the 50s and 60s – *Reach for the Sky, The Dam Busters, The Bridge on the River Kwai, Doctor Zhivago,* and of course those wonderful *Carry On* films – made a deep and lasting impression on me. Unsurprisingly, you will find references to them dotted throughout this book.

Conventional saleroom auctions offer little scope for thespianisms inspired by my dramatic tastes. Though I have developed a passable imitation of Kenneth More's Douglas Bader, for example, it is strictly for private viewing and not for the rostrum. That said, I endeavour to involve the audience in the proceedings as much as possible and seek to add a bit of zip with the occasional quip. Nonetheless, it's still more sermon than standup.

Charity auctions are a different matter altogether. At these events I am free, within limits, to use the rostrum as a starting point for a bit of pantomime. I have no script; a few well-tried tropes, perhaps, but nothing planned in advance and certainly nothing on paper. A Charlie Ross charity auction, controlled chaos with a smile, is impromptu. Something like this ...

I'm on the podium selling two tickets for a show. At a table to my right sit a middle-aged couple muttering urgently to each other. It's clear what's happening: she, a couple of glasses of Chablis this side of Leighton Buzzard, is eager to bid £1,500 for two tickets to *My Fair Lady* at the Oxford Playhouse as a birthday present for her daughter; he, driving home and therefore on the ginger beer, loves their daughter just as much but thinks fifteen hundred quid is a bit steep for a show with tickets normally going for £100.

Impasse.

Planted on the rostrum, having questioned and cajoled without success, I prepare to bring the hammer down at £1,400. Then something takes hold of me. I'm sure, if I could talk to the man face to face, I'd be able to get him to support his wife's exorbitant bid. The fundraisers need the cash. But he's twenty feet away and not looking at me.

Instinct takes over. Leaving the sanctuary of the dais and venturing among the audience is a high-risk manoeuvre; it can be used only sparingly and only at charity auctions, but it invariably works. Here goes ...

I seize the roving mic, leap down from the rostrum, and

run up to the wavering husband.

'Sir, you know you have come to a charity auction?' He nods and gives a half-smile.

'And can you and your wife afford the pittance, the mere trifle, she is prepared to bid for these tickets?'

I know from their clothes, shoes and jewellery – let alone the price they have paid for this fundraising dinner – that they can.

'Maybe, Charlie,' he replies sheepishly. 'Just about.' The audience laughs and applauds.

'Then come along, sir. Be a latter-day Sir Galahad and support the lady in distress on your left. And in doing so give [whatever the charity is] a tremendous boost.'

More laughter and cries of 'Go on!' etc from the audience. As he is still hesitating, I turn to his wife.

'Madam, is he normally like this?'

She roars with laughter. 'Only sometimes!'

'And this is one of those times?'

'I hope not!'

That does it. Collapse of stout party. 'Alright then. Go ahead!'

Back to the podium I dash. 'Thank you, sir; thank you, madam. You have made a lot of people happy and helped a truly worthy cause with your generosity. Now, two tickets for *My Fair Lady* at one thousand five hundred pounds for the first time …'

A friend of mine once described antics like this as "athletic auctioneering". It's true that, like a good deal of theatre, they involve vigorous physical activity. I sprint back and forth several times between tables and the rostrum, losing (to Sally's delight) several pounds in weight in a single evening. I'm fortunate in having a constitution able to handle all this. We don't have a gym at home, and though I did once manage the Great North Run (for charity), my sole exercise apart from charity auctions is on the golf course or raising glasses of the Wine Society's delicious Chateau Pitray.

Athletic genes run in the family. My father was a fine swimmer who, until sixty-Embassy-a-day filled his lungs with black treacle, could swim more lengths of a pool underwater than the average person could manage on the surface. My mother was an excellent gymnast who was obliged to give up the sport when, in her own words, she became 'too top-heavy'. I remember her as an 85-year-old sitting in the back seat of a car complaining that 'I can no longer do *this*' – and then proceeding to show us what 'this' was by swinging a leg up and over the driver's seat.

Family trips to athletics meetings at the White City Stadium (built for the 1908 Olympics, demolished 1985) were a regular summer event. The memory's a bit hazy at this distance but names like Gordon Pirie and Derek Ibbotson float into view. In a strange sort of tribute to them, when Stewart and I raced back from The Old Red Lion in Great Brickhill one of us was Pirie and the other Ibbotson. Drifting through the mists of time is also the unmistakable voice of commentator Norris McWhirter, co-founder of *The Guinness Book of Records*. In another odd tribute to past heroes, my brother and I often refer to each other as "Norris" (myself) and "McWhirter" (Stewart). The next generation has picked up on this, my nephew naming his dog Norris, though I am not sure this is a compliment.

At school, cricket was my favourite sport – and it still is, which is why it has a chapter all to itself (Fourteen). I also participated, with a greater or lesser degree of success, in a wide variety of other athletic activities. Not that I necessarily wanted to. At our delightful Dotheboys institution, being sent on a run was a popular punishment meted out by prefects. 'Three times round the castle, Ross!' or, worst of all, 'Ashley Green – and back by prep or you're for it!' Ashley

Green, a small village some miles from the school, was reached by running ('I'm watching, Ross!') up a very steep hill. I can't remember how long it took to get there and back: over an hour, certainly.

Formal athletics (track and field) was more enjoyable, probably because I was quite good at it. I could sprint reasonably fast and as I matured I developed those substantial thighs (featured in Chapter Three) that enabled me to leap like a gazelle into the long jump pit. Alas, whatever gazelle-like qualities I might once have possessed have long since withered: the other day I measured out my longest ever jump in the back garden and couldn't believe how far it was – nearly twice the length of my car!

School athletics was run by our lop-eared house tutor, the same man who chastised my brother for talking to me and who punished me for being late back one Sunday after my father's car had a puncture. He approached sport as he did everything else, including the English literature that he taught, with unyielding vigour. Wearing gigantic white shorts that billowed like spinnakers, and shod in size 13 plimsoll shoes, he participated personally in all training. 'Right-o! Follow me!' and off he went round the grass track like a human ostrich. Plimsolls, for the uninitiated, are the thin-soled, omni-purpose ancestor of the modern trainer, sneaker or pump, that once served for just about every school sport apart from rugby and football. Only in my final year of athletics did I graduate to spiked running shoes.

Rugby – or "rugger" as it was known – was compulsory at school. This was fine for large, beefy types like Stewart who didn't mind throwing themselves at the muddied and studded feet of the opposition, but for timid characters such as myself trudging half a mile up the hill to the sports field in the pouring rain on a cold January afternoon, and then being trampled underfoot or howled at for an hour because I had not "gone low" was not enjoyable. The athletic side of it was alright and if, on a dry spring day, I found myself with ball in hand and no one in front of me, I could run like the wind – at least, it felt like the wind: there was a lot of it on those elevated fields. Somebody saw me on one of these speedy forays and put me in the 2nd XV. That was the apex of my school rugby career.

That it was not the apex of my whole rugby career was due to Richard Smith, a friend I made while working in Buckingham. I was in Johnson's office one damp autumn day, staring out of the window and not thinking of much, when in burst Richard.

'Rosco, old boy! The 3rd XV needs you!' Richard was a farmer, hence the genial, no-nonsense manner.

'Er, what?'

'Come off it! You said you'd played rugby at school, so you know the rules. We need you to play for us.'

'Who's "us"?'

'Buckingham 3rds. Great team. Match on Saturday against Wolverton. Don't let us down, Rosco.'

I couldn't and didn't. On Saturday we met up with David Spicer, another player, and warmed up with three pints of Hook Norton (splendid ale, though on the strong side) in The King's Head, Chackmore. From there David drove us to Wolverton, where we changed in a building resembling a cross between a cowshed and a Nissen hut and took to the field. The player opposite me, another farmer, looked the sort that trained by running across a ploughed field with a fully grown pig under each arm, and I hoped the ball would not come in my direction any time soon.

It didn't, not because it wasn't passed or kicked towards me, but because the game came to a screaming (literally) halt before it had hardly started. The ball was dropped at kick-off (normal 3rd XV practice) and the ref called a scrum. The forwards engaged – then disengaged – in a cacophony of swearing and finger pointing. The target was David Spicer. I walked over to investigate. Had he punched someone? No, his crime was far more original: he had gone into the scrum with a lighted cigar clamped between his teeth and pointing directly at his opposite number in the front row. The poor fellow saw the approaching red glow too late for evasive action and it sizzled into his cheek!

The forwards grumbled and swore before eventually agreeing with the ref that the game could continue only if David apologised and extinguished his cigar. I retreated back to the wing. What on earth had I let myself in for? Nothing even remotely like this had ever happened in a school rugby match.

As it turned out, the Spicer cigar incident was a one-off. Buckingham Rugby Club made me very welcome, and I spent several happy years playing on the wing for various teams, including, on occasion, their illustrious 1st XV. My speed enabled me to score sufficient tries for my deficiencies in defence to be overlooked – but not forgotten. They gave me the nickname ET, not because I looked like a little green monster from outer space but because I was Excused Tackling.

Anyone who has played rugby (or any team sport) for any length of time can come up with a litany of anecdotes – some amusing, others smutty, many best forgotten – so I'll limit mine to just three, concluding with an addendum on why I gave up playing. Story One concerns the game stopped by the arrival of a police car. Two officers got out and asked if we had Kevin Old with us. Yes, we did, our captain replied. He was the full back. Not for long. Kevin was escorted off the pitch in handcuffs and taken down to the station. We carried on with fourteen men – and lost.

Story Two concerns another missing player. We were due

to kick off against Henley, a much more prosperous club than Buckingham, when we were told that their fullback had failed to show up. We made appropriately sympathetic noises but agreed with the referee's decision that the game should begin without him. We started well and were on the point of making our numerical advantage tell when the ref blew his whistle and pointed to the sky. A minute or so later, a private helicopter landed in the middle of the pitch. Out jumped a man dressed in rugby kit, number 15 on his back: the opposition's fullback. He was rather good, too, and again we lost by a wide margin.

Any collection of rugby tales generally has two essential features: drink and New Zealand. My Story Three has both. Buckingham Rugby Club regularly attracted visiting Kiwis looking for a game. One of these was a likeable fellow named Chris Blane aka Blaney, an enthusiastic player – when sober. The problem was keeping him off the bottle until after the match. One day he turned up at a tournament so drunk that he couldn't remember his position or catch the ball.

'Wha'shall I do?' he asked the captain.

'Oh, I don't know, Blaney. Just tackle the first person you see moving.'

Blaney took him at his word. Unfortunately, the man who came into his sights was Jonny Johnson, the top-class referee allocated to our match that afternoon. He had just blown his whistle for the start of the game before – THUMP! – Blaney sent him sprawling onto the turf. Instant red card and, of course, we lost another match.

The art of making a proper rugby tackle involves three things: (1) wrap your arms around the player you are tackling, (2) bash them between chest and knee with your shoulder, and (3) keep your head well out of the way. I was not very good at no 1, pretty poor at no 2, and utterly hopeless at no 3. On the couple of occasions when I tried really, really hard to get all three right, I still failed to master the what-to-do-with-your-head bit. At least, I'm told that's what happened – my memories of each occasion are a total blank.

On New Year's Eve 1971, I was playing rugby for the town of Leighton Buzzard (I've no idea why) when I made my first attempt at a tri-pronged international-class tackle and was knocked out cold. Someone took me home (I was still living with my parents at the time and they were still living with each other) and put to bed muttering, 'Who won? Who won?'

My mother and father then went out for the evening. Half an hour later, the front doorbell rang. I blinked, rose woozily to my feet, pulled on a dressing gown and went downstairs. On opening the front door, I found my girlfriend Diana and the Suter brothers, two of my best mates. All three were dressed in formal evening wear.

'Come on Charlie! What are you playing at? You're late!'

'Who won?'

'Oh shut up and get dressed!'

Somehow I did, and off we went (thank God I was not driving) to the Hogmanay party thrown by Alexander Hesketh (now Lord Hesketh). Actually, it was a ball, not a party, extremely formal and very smart. (Hesketh was inordinately wealthy and went on to set up his own Formula 1 racing team, Hesketh-Ford, starring James Hunt, aka "Hunt the Shunt".) In the impressive entry hall, we were greeted by an announcer in smart red livery.

'Name, sir?'

'Who won?'

Diana had by this time realised that something was amiss and persuaded him not to announce a Chinese gentleman, "Mr Charles Hoowun". However, she could not prevent me joining the queue to be introduced to Alexander's mother, Lady Hesketh.

'Ah, you must be Diana's friend – how lovely to meet you.'

'Who won?'

With that, I was taken home and put back to bed.

Ten years later, now a married man, I made my second attempt at an international-class tackle, and once again was knocked out cold. I was taken off the pitch and sat staring blankly at the mud-splattered clubhouse wall until the match finished. Dick the Doc, our GP and an enthusiastic supporter, kindly agreed to drive me home. I left my car at the ground to be collected when I was in a fit state to drive.

'Where to, Charlie?'

'That's really good of you, Dick: Drive Cottage, Akeley Wood.'

On arrival, I got out of the car and went to the front door. *Keys? Damn, I must have left them in my car back at the ground.* I knocked and waited with my friend beside me. A smiling American lady opened the door.

'Charlie! Good to see you!'

'Mrs Ross, I'm afraid Charlie's got concussion,' Dick explained, 'and I thought it best to bring him home.'

'Home? Well, for a start I'm not Mrs Ross, and Charlie and Sally haven't lived here for over a year!'

The next day, Dick told me that I'd either have to give up rugby football or change doctors. Sally made the decision for me.

CHAPTER SEVEN

Downer Ross

By the age of thirty-two, I felt I had finally put my A-Level fiasco and dreams of dentistry behind me. I lived in a delightful old house (shortly to be Grade II listed) with a lovely family; my bread-and-butter auctions met the cost of the mortgage, and a bit of dealing in antiques and the occasional extra auction paid for summer holidays and deliveries from The Wine Society. And yet ...

Driving to the Finchley auction every week, I often sang along to my favourite music. 'Wouldn't it be loverly' I chimed, fairly tunefully, alongside Eliza Doolittle as she imagined herself in a warm room beside a roaring fire in *My Fair Lady*. I echoed her words, but not her dream. Mine was to have a saleroom of my own so I did not have to hawk myself around like a gavel-armed knight errant selling my services at other people's courts. Auctioneering is a precarious occupation, too. Like Julie Andrews, the first Eliza Doolittle, all I had was my voice. (Not strictly true; she had a quiver full of other qualities – film-star good looks for a start – not evident on my CV.) Nevertheless, by the early 1980s, I had my bread and butter and a little jam – what I now needed was a plate to put it on.

Plates, however, are expensive.

In the Westerns that held Stewart and me spellbound in our youth, there was always a moment when, over the brow of the hill, John Wayne rode to the rescue. On this occasion my rescuer was no John Wayne. As I suggested in Chapter Three, Alan Downer, my old friend and colleague from W.S. Johnson & Co., did not come booted and spurred, and he arrived in a Jaguar rather than on horseback. No matter, he reappeared on the scene at the most opportune moment.

'Charlie, old boy,' he said on the phone one day in 1983, 'I have a proposition to make to you. How about a spot of lunch?' I accepted, though not without some trepidation as I remembered my adventure with Avril Magwitch-Klein. Surely Alan wasn't going to offer me another Aussie escort? He wasn't.

I mentioned at the beginning of these misty recollections that luck, unlike lightning, can strike more than once. I had already been a rod for a flash of fortune on several occasions, and lunch with Alan proved to be yet another.

'What I'm thinking, Charlie,' he began, 'is that we ought to set up some sort of partnership.'

His remark took a while to sink in. The word "partnership" had thrown me. At the time it had a trendy new meaning ... no, that certainly wasn't what Alan meant. That left only one possibility – partnership in the business sense. Impossible, surely?

Being an ingénu in the world of business-speak, I nodded in what I hoped was a knowing manner. 'What sort of partnership did you have in mind, Alan?'

'Well, Charlie, old boy, what I have in mind is this ...'

Alan had left W.S. Johnson & Co a while back and was now a senior partner in a firm of surveyors and estate agents in Milton Keynes. Knowing that the antiques market was booming and believing I knew a little bit about it, he thought it would be a smart idea for his business to have a saleroom attached. As an 'experienced and accomplished auctioneer' (a flattering phrase he backed up by reminding me that in my Bletchley days I had won the RICS Berks, Bucks and Oxon Young Auctioneer of the Year competition), would I like to run the saleroom side of things as a partner of his firm and help with the bookkeeping in the Milton Keynes office?

Partnership? I thought that had gone out of the window, carried away on the same breeze that had blown away my chances of joining the RICS when I made a hash of their final exams. Partnership in a flourishing enterprise *and* my own saleroom – surely this was too good to be true? I was confident that my thirty-four-year-old O-Level in advanced mathematics could handle a bit of book-keeping.

Remembering just in time that bona fide businesspeople always take a long, deep breath before making a decision, I thanked Alan for his kind offer and said I'd give it serious thought and come back to him in a couple of days. I couldn't wait. Two days shrank to one, then twelve hours … six hours, and I rang him that evening to accept. Thus was Downer Ross Fine Art Auctioneers born. The name order was not simply alphabetical: the business could not have got off the ground without the financial backing that Alan was able to conjure up.

My partnership was up and running but did not yet have a suitable saleroom, a base from which to operate. Milton Keynes being a city built from scratch, there were plenty of shiny new premises but Alan and I agreed that plate glass and concrete cows would not be an appropriate background against which to display items whose value usually depended on their age. As Alan succinctly put it, the shiny metropolis of rigid lines and concrete cows 'lacked woodworm'. Not that the furniture we had for sale was riddled, but I knew what he meant.

When clearing the way for their new city, the Milton Keynes Development Corporation did not bulldoze all existing buildings. Those of historical, cultural and aesthetic interest were retained, small islands of heritage in a sea of contemporaneity. One of these islands was Great Linford Manor, an impressive 17th-century house built on the site of its medieval predecessor and acquired by the Corporation as an arts centre in 1972. Alan and I went to have a look.

Yes, it was just the sort of prestigious building we were looking for, and Alan negotiated with the Corporation for permission to hold an auction there twice a year. We spread the word among the antiques fraternity that Downer Ross was launching a new and exciting series of sales in Milton Keynes, the first of their kind in that city. To our relief – and somewhat to my surprise – the idea caught on and our first catalogue was quite impressive.

Its centrepiece was a dresser base in yew wood from The Green Man pub in Syresham. In 2024 we may well wonder why anyone would want an incomplete piece of furniture in anything so unexceptional as yew. Surely the primary purpose of this bendy wood was making bows for Robin Hood, not dressers? What was going on?

The market for rare pieces of Tudor and Jacobean pieces had always been strong, as it had been for the elegance of Chippendale, Sheraton and their French contemporaries. What was new during the 1970s and most of the 1980s was the booming market for all items of "brown" furniture. Brown here refers to items made from heavy, dark-coloured wood. Oak and mahogany come first, with walnut, rosewood and other hard woods not far behind. The boom was partly a matter of fashion and partly a reaction to the growing rarity (and consequent price rise) of these pillars of the world's dwindling forests.

Where there is a boom, criminality is never far behind, and the antiques world was no exception. Enter "the ring". The crooked and illegal practice works like this:

1. a group of buyers (dealers and others with a nose for a dodgy deal) meet to study the items featuring in a forthcoming sale

2. they choose pieces which can do well if sold in the right market but which are unlikely to appeal to the average buyer or whose value is often underestimated (eg an unexceptional-looking piece that could be attributed to a specific cabinet maker)

3. they might have a market for the item in mind already (eg an overseas buyer)

4. at the auction, one ring member bids while the others hang fire, giving the ring purchaser a good chance of getting the target piece at well below its true market value

5. the ring then holds an illegal closed auction, known as a "knock-out", among themselves

6. the profit – the difference between the price paid at the legal auction and that paid at the knock-out – is shared between ring members

This shady dealing is, or certainly used to be, difficult to call out, and only a few rings were prosecuted. An auctioneer, myself included, might be wary when lots went for suspiciously low prices, but malpractice could not be proved without concrete evidence and that was extremely hard to come by. Knowing nods and winks were not enough.

'Got yourself a bit of a bargain there, Norman?'

'Yes, Charlie. I was in luck. Nobody else seemed to want it.'

Oh yes? So what about that weasel-faced bloke at the back of the saleroom? He seemed pretty interested when looking round the lots yesterday afternoon, so I wonder why he didn't bid? Perhaps you had a chat with him in The King's Head last night ... I might think it, but I couldn't say it.

Two developments have made rings much harder to operate. One is the spread of telephone and online bidding; the other is professionalized cataloguing. Nowadays, few sales worth their salt take place without phone bids and detailed, historically accurate catalogue descriptions together with reserve prices and estimated sale prices. As a consequence, artificial bargains are thankfully now rare.

I have explained ring fraud because I learned later that a ring was interested in the yew dresser base that was the pièce de résistance in our first sale. The shenanigans failed only because the ringleader missed the bidding as he dashed to hospital with a ring member who had fallen ill. In their absence, the piece sold for a tidy £2,300. Downer Ross was up and running.

Though Great Linford Manor was a splendid setting for an auction of old things, our presence in what was in effect the Milton Keynes Arts Centre was both precarious (the Corporation would soon sell the site for private use) and awkward. Georgian card tables did not sit easily with yoga classes and exhibitions of amateur acrylics. After a couple of sales, we were looking around for a more secure and appropriate base.

I had known the small town of Woburn most of my life and had often driven past its neo-Jacobean red-brick Town Hall without taking much notice. Now I looked more carefully. The setting was ideal: a charming small Georgian town with broad streets and a history that could be traced back to the *Doomsday Book* of 1086. The only possible drawback was the etymology of the place: "Woburn" originated with "woe burn" or "crooked stream", hardly ideal for someone who promised to conduct business in a scrupulously straight manner. Fortunately, my clients were not antiquarians and the misalignment was never commented upon.

The town hall could hardly have been bettered: Grade II listed, eye-catching position, good-sized car park nearby, numerous period features, spacious assembly room on the 1st floor … you can tell I had been an estate agent, can't you? As this was to be my base for the next twenty-five years, perhaps a little background would not come amiss.

In the late 1820s, when an English Revolution was a very real possibility, the more prudent members of the governing classes were taking steps to hasten reform and divert attention from their positions of opulent privilege. One such was the Whig magnate John Russell, 6th Duke of Bedford, owner of nearby Woburn Abbey which Henry VIII had given to the family in 1538. A great fan of Napoleon Bonaparte, Duke John had funded pamphlets criticising Britain's wars with revolutionary France and declared openly that he hoped Wellington's Peninsular campaign would end in failure!

Back at home, the duke did his bit for the local population by pulling down the decrepit old town hall and gifting Woburn with a splendid new one, for which he charged no rent (how times have changed!). The architect was the fashionable Edward Blore (1787–1879), who had already made a name for himself by designing an exotic palace in Crimea – half-Scottish, half-Arab – for a Russian prince. He went on to work on various English cathedrals, Windsor Castle, and the façade of Buckingham Palace overlooking The Mall. King George V would be so offended by the latter, apparently calling it 'banal street architecture', that he had it remodelled along the lines we are familiar with today.

Nobody, as far as I know, has castigated Woburn Town Hall as street architecture. Neither Downer nor Ross thought it banal, either. We loved the place, especially the assembly room on the first floor with its oriel window, vaulted ceiling (acoustically excellent) and panel emblazoned with the arms of the Russell family. The antiques writer John Rumens once paid us a visit and described the place "as pretty a venue as you could wish". He was less impressed with the "patchy" lighting and "less than healthy" loos. We had to agree with him – at the time both issues were out of our hands.

Our initial contract gave us the hall for one five-day week in every month. This meant auction week was a bit of a scramble.

Monday: Arrival of lots. Hundreds of them, some from Alan's garage that we had accumulated over the previous three weeks, a few pieces from dealers and private individuals, and the rest from houses we had cleared. All had to be lugged upstairs and set out, more or less higgledy-piggledy, in the assembly hall/saleroom.

Tuesday: "Lotting up". Describing the items for sale, giving them a lot number, and arranging them around the Hall in as attractive a manner as possible. At the same time, lot numbers and brief descriptions ("Lot 147. Dinky Toy Fire Engine, c.1956, boxed, good condition") were assembled into a hand-written then typed and Gestetnered catalogue. No pictures in the early days.

Wednesday: Viewing day. Into the saleroom came all kinds of bargain hunter, ranging from Barbour-wearing dealers to tweedy couples from small antiques shops, and young couples hoping to furnish their home on the cheap. Alan and I answered questions to the best of our ability.

Thursday: Sale day. On the day of his visit, John Rumens described it being conducted by a man "with a receding tan, a bold blue shirt and a dashing manner" whose voice rebounded off the turquoise walls of the saleroom with "astonishing clarity". I wonder who he was referring to?

Friday: Removal day. Purchasers had twenty-four hours to collect their treasures. Uncollected lots were taken back to Alan's garage for future collection.

At this stage, the average reader may well be wondering about saleroom economics. During a good sale, a lot of money changes hands very quickly: 'Cash or cheque will do nicely madam. No, I'm sorry, but it has to be today.' Where does this money come from and where does it go?

A traditional auction was simple. The vendor entered an object in the sale, with or without a reserve price. If the item sold, the purchaser paid the "hammer price" (that reached when the bidding ends) immediately. The auctioneers passed this money to the vendor, less a percentage (generally around 15%) agreed beforehand. So if your item sold for £1,000, you received £850 and the auction house £150.

The process became more complicated with the advent of VAT (1973) and the "buyer's premium" (see below), as well as eBay and other online platforms. Even before these developments, the advantages of selling at auction were not always clear.

On several occasions, I have been approached by someone asking why, if they can get a decent price at a conventional sale, they should bother putting an item up for auction. The answer is straightforward: competition. Almost no tangible object has intrinsic value; it is worth only what someone is prepared to pay for it. That can best be ascertained at auction, when one learns how far interested parties are prepared to go. For a modest fee, an auction house will value an item, advertise it, and do their best to find a buyer. And one can play safe by putting a reserve price on it, too. What's to lose?

Unfortunately, in September 1975, the modern auction

business became more complicated. Two of the great London houses, Christie's and Sotheby's, announced that they were deepening their research into items they offered for sale. The purpose, they argued, was to clarify the provenance of the items they had for sale and therefore take some of the risk out of bidding. How thoughtful of them!

Not so fast ... Deepening research and setting it out in a more elaborate catalogue cost the auction houses money. Where could it come from? As they were already charging the vendor, the purchaser remained the only possible source of extra revenue. Enter the buyer's premium, a charge (anything from ten to thirty percent) on the hammer price. The premium also attracted VAT.

As a consequence, someone buying an item for £1,000 found themselves being asked for £1,000 plus a premium of X% + VAT. The surcharge understandably attracted widespread criticism, not least from Lord Cocks of Hartcliffe in a debate in the House of Lords on 20 June 1991.

> When I was a boy, that [charging a buyer's premium] would have been described as having one's cake and eating it. In Bristol we have a more homely phrase. We call it having the penny and the bun. Either way it seems that there is a clear dichotomy between the auction house acting as agent for the seller and being charged with obtaining the best price and, in addition, exacting a payment from the purchaser.

His lordship's pained appeal for a ban on the buyer's premium fell on the deaf ears of his fellow peers.

The development presented Downer Ross and similar-sized auction houses with a problem: where Christie's and Sotheby's had led, should we follow by introducing a buyer's premium? Alan and I thought long and hard, and eventually fell back on the oldest schoolboy excuse: everybody else was doing it, so why shouldn't we? Not extravagantly, though, just a modest five percent. At a time when catalogues were getting smarter, featuring numerous photographs and coloured covers, a little extra income came in handy. I blush to admit that our lowly percentage lasted no longer than snow on the desert face: neither rents nor wages freeze for long, and the brown furniture boom had to end at some time, so up went our premium. To help sweeten the pill, and the saleroom atmosphere, we even smartened up our lavatories.

Running a saleroom in the days before readily affordable computers, photocopiers and printers was slow, painstaking work. Our illustrated catalogue, for instance, was a marathon task. The initial text was handwritten by me or Alan's wife Rosemary, and the semi-legible scrawl, criss-crossed with arrows and asterisks, handed to our remarkable saleroom secretary, Donna Watling. Donna was the Usain Bolt of the keyboard, rattling the keys at Gatling speed to produce a faultless catalogue of over five hundred lots, Gestetner-ready, in a little over five hours. Once it had been run off back in the Milton Keynes office, it fell to our saleroom manager, Evan Willison, and me to glue the three-hundred-odd pictures in by hand.

Rosemary, Donna, Evan and I were the catalogue team. Behind us, underpinning the whole business, stood the most efficient woman in the world. Venetia Frost ran the office, kept the books, paid the bills, and did the thousand-and-one jobs that kept the business running smoothly. If this makes Venetia sound like a robot, you should have seen her at the Downer Ross Christmas party. Boring Venetia was not!

We – me, Alan, and all the staff – worked on a sort of family basis. No one had a contract. Instead, everyone did what was necessary to make the business a success. If that meant working late, so be it. If, on the other hand, someone wanted to leave early or have a day off for some reason, then that was fine.

Evan Willison set the tone. Surely there was no finer saleroom manager in the country? He combined the work of a Trojan with the eye of a South Ken interior designer: no matter what ill-assorted jumble of goods piled into the saleroom at the beginning of the week, by the day of the sale he had it looking like the drawing room of a large manor house.

Paintings in ornate gilt frames, three-hundred-year-old wooden furniture, delicate fine bone china – antiques and objets d'art require very careful handling. Here, too, Evan excelled. I once asked him where he had learned to be so careful with the items he was carrying.

'You forget, Charlie, I was an ambulance driver before I started this job.'

'But you don't have to be too careful lugging patients about, do you?'

'You do when you're delivering them to the person I had to.'

'Oh yes? Who was it?'

'Your mother!'

Ah! That explained it. My mother had trained as a physiotherapist in Guy's Hospital at a time when such institutions were run along the lines parodied by Hattie Jacques and James Robertson Justice in *Carry On Doctor*. The clinic she headed in Bletchley was no place for the faint-hearted.

'You deliver a patient, Mr Willison, as you would a baby. Would you dare drop a baby?'

'No, Mrs Ross. Never.'

'Then don't drop my patients.'

My mother could be like that sometimes.

Evan had a fine sense of humour, too. If Alan's watchword in stressful times was, 'Have another gin and tonic, old boy,' Evan's was 'Leave it to me, Charlie.' And I did, most memorably in the short two-hand drama based on the visit of a Health and Safety Officer.

Evan discovered on stage, polishing silver.
Enter stage left Health and Safety Officer.
OFFICER (*pompously*): May I see your accident book, sir?
EVAN (*still polishing*): I beg your pardon?
OFFICER: I asked if I might see your accident book, sir.
EVAN (*looking up*): Accident book?
OFFICER: Yes, accident book.
EVAN (*resumes polishing*): We don't have one.
OFFICER: Ah, so what do you do if there's an accident?
Evan stops polishing and thinks for a moment.
EVAN: Well, if it's really bad I go to hospital. (*Resumes polishing.*) If it's not, I bandage it up and carry on working.
OFFICER: Really?
EVAN (*polishing even harder*): Yes, really. Common sense.
OFFICER (*after a pause*): Well, yes. I suppose it is.
Exit stage right Health and Safety Officer, never to return.

The episode of Evan and the HSO illustrates more than the saleroom manager's cheerful, cheeky personality; it encapsulated Downer Ross. We were, I hope, efficient and fair without being grasping or putting profit before people. It would be too clichéd to describe us as a happy family, though that is what it felt like to work there. No one went on strike or, as far as I recall, left to go to another job. At its simplest, our guiding principles were to make a living and have fun – and not always in that order.

Which brings me to the subject of auctioneering. The primary purpose of an auctioneer is to get the highest possible price for each lot. This is, if one thinks about it, an awesome responsibility: one wrong word, even an ill-directed nod, can have serious consequences: the loss of large sums of money, acrimony and even legal action in the more extreme cases. Awareness of this portentous responsibility can lead many to wield the gavel with extreme caution and seriousness – we have all seen them in action during the well-publicised sale of an impressive piece of art in one of the famous auction houses: slow, deliberate, deadpan, crystal clear and cautious.

That's not how auctions worked at Downer Ross, and not how I conduct any of my auctions elsewhere, even when handling $15 million Ferraris. Worthy seriousness, as personified by my civil servant grandfather who worked (10 am–3.30 pm) for the Inland Revenue in Somerset House, is not in my nature. I identify more closely with his son, John, who is said to have displayed considerable dramatic talent as a schoolboy. (Unlike me, who hadn't the courage to mess with Shakespeare, John apparently veered seriously off-piste in the Macbeth murder scene by pointing at the dagger and saying in broad Yorkshire, 'Eee by gum, it's all covered in blood!') By the time John reached the age of eighteen, my grandfather despaired of ever shepherding him into a safe career. In a move of kindly but rare speculation, he gave his son enough money for a passage to Hollywood where he could make a name for himself. Unfortunately, the life-changing trip to California got no further than the local pub where John threw a five-star farewell party. When he woke up the following morning and turned his pockets inside out, he found he had no money left for his ticket to the US.

Had he not been shot down and killed in 1943, John might have made a fine if unconventional auctioneer.

So might my father if his maths had been better and the cards had fallen the right way for him. He was by all accounts very amusing on stage, notably starring as a

Chaplin-style comedian in *Bumpkin Pie*, an amateur pantomime/revue staged in Newton Blossomville around 1954. I was too young to attend but Stewart remembers "Pa" bringing the house down.

When on the rostrum, I do not want to bring the house down. On the other hand, nor do I want the audience to switch or, worse still, nod off. A room full of people focussing on the single figure on a stage is too precious an opportunity for it to be only about money. It's an occasion, a piece of tragi-comic live drama with real characters involved in a high-tension who'll-get-it plot.

As the leading actor, I try to make the show as entertaining as possible without trivialising or losing sight of my prime purpose – ie get the best price for the lots in the catalogue. It's a truism but still worth remembering, as the managers of Disney World and karaoke evenings will testify, that people are more likely to spend freely if they are enjoying themselves. My idea of a good time, however, is not necessarily yours; like an actor or standup comedian, an auctioneer, especially one who likes to have fun, has to know their audience. Though offering to lend a tenner to a hesitant bidder gets a laugh at a charity auction, it would not go down well with the steely-eyed exiles attending the Russian art sales I used to conduct in London.

I'm getting ahead of myself. Back to Downer Ross Fine Art Auctioneers, Woburn. We had a fine saleroom, excellent staff and two competent auctioneers: all we now needed was something to sell.

CHAPTER EIGHT

Clearing Houses

The community of professional antiques dealers and salerooms is small and tight knit. News of Downer Ross's move to Woburn Town Hall soon got around, and we had little difficulty attracting interest in our new premises and its eclectic contents. Most of our early stock, including a few quite special pieces, came from house clearances.

Undertakers and auctioneers have two things in common. They understand that once the hammer has fallen there's no going back, and they share a common interest in house clearances. The latter is potentially very profitable. However, as it is invariably the consequence of a personal tragedy – perhaps only people leaving to join a religious order are disinterested in the fate of their worldly possessions – it requires tactful and sympathetic handling. In my experience, divorces are the most trying, deaths the most harrowing, and bankruptcies the saddest (usually because those losing their home, as in my mother's case, have had little or no say in what has brought this about).

For dealers with a faulty moral compass, house

clearances also present an opportunity for crooked behaviour.

Your grandfather may have *told* you that he brought that old vase back from China when he was in the Navy, but I see things like that every day. Take my word for it, Mr Wilkins, your grandfather picked it up in a junk shop in Portsmouth after getting off the ship. Got "Made in Manchester" written all over it. The factory in Chapel Street churned 'em out by the thousands. Worth a tenner at best.

I hope it is unnecessary to assure you that this was not the way of Downer Ross, though I would not put that sort of behaviour past some of those I came across. I like to think we managed our business with honesty, tact and efficiency. Alan, as befitted a dealer in fine old furniture, was French polish smooth, and I have never enjoyed offending people. Our staff provided the efficiency. Most of the time.

Mick Stevens, who resembled an elongated version of the actor Charles Hawtrey, was one of our regular and most trusted porters. His everyday job was farming at Bovingdon near Berkhamsted, which always surprised me. To this day, I struggle to imagine him delivering lambs on frosty evenings or supping a mug of foaming scrumpy on top of a hay wagon. But perhaps that's not how farming is anymore?

Anyway, when he came to lend a hand on viewing and sale days, Mick was the epitome of professionalism. He assured me that, 'What goes on in the saleroom stays in the saleroom.' We didn't have anything to hide, but if we had it was reassuring to know that it was safe with Mick.

Downer Ross also benefitted from Mick's third job: proprietor of a removal and delivery business. One of his principal clients was John Bly, the TV antiques expert. Having inherited a flourishing business in Tring, John appeared regularly on the BBC's *Antiques Roadshow* where his pinstripe suits and crisp, good-humoured observations made him quite a star.

Given Mick's reliability and experience with antiques, we trusted him completely. With good reason. A true story doing the rounds on the antiques circuit at the time is a perfect example of his unswerving professionalism.

Flatt & Mead, a Berkhamsted estate agent with its own auction room, asked Mick to clear an apartment that had been vacated when its elderly owner moved into a nursing home. The agents had previously inspected the flat and valued both it and the contents. They planned to put the flat on the market the next day, empty of all furniture.

'No problem,' said Mick. 'Leave it to me.' And they did.

Mick picked up the keys from Flatt & Mead, collected a mate of his to help, and drove round to the apartment in one of his capacious vans. In three hours the two men had cleared out the entire contents – dining table, beds, books, fridge, food, toilet rolls and all. When they had finished, only the fitted carpets and curtains remained, as the estate agents had stipulated.

Mick then drove back to the Flatt & Mead saleroom and started to unload. He hadn't got far before Adrian Harris, the company's saleroom manager and the man who had valued the flat and its contents, arrived to check that all was going according to plan.

After greeting Mick, he stood and watched with increasing bewilderment as the items were carried out of the van. One red Formica-topped table ... red? One sofa in green velour ... green velour? A box of assorted cutlery with imitation ivory handles ...

'Er, Mick?'

'Yes. Adrian?'

'You did clear number 18, didn't you?'

'Number 18? No, of course not. I was given the keys to 16.'

Adrian turned pale. 'What the ****! You've cleared the wrong bloody flat!'

The two of them hurried back to the office where it soon became clear what had happened. Both flats, 16 and 18, were for sale with Flatt & Mead. The keys to each hung side by side on the key rack. When Mick asked for the keys of 'the flat in Manor Street', he was handed those of 16 instead of 18. A simple mistake with potentially very costly consequences.

The crisis saw Mick at his best.

Within five minutes, he, his helper and Adrian have reloaded the van and are roaring back to Manor Street. They approach the flats cautiously – had the resident of no 16 returned? No! Thank God! Right, let's get to work!

Four hours later, flat 16 is in precisely the same state as when the owner left for work that morning. The food is back in the fridge, the easy chairs are pulled up before the gas fire, and the toilet roll is back in its holder. The flat next door, no 18, stands empty and its contents are safely packed into Mick's van.

And the most astonishing part of the story? The owner of flat 16 returned home that evening, cooked supper, watched TV, probably used the toilet, and went to bed without realising for one second what had happened. I gather he was never told, even after Flatt & Mead had negotiated the sale of his property – including its contents!

The chap who was with Mick at the time of the Flatt & Mead escapade was one of several co-porters he used to help out at sale time. He was also helped by Dave Roberts, one of Evan's friends. Dave is a jovial, comfortable-looking man with a mop of hay-coloured hair whose second-hand shop in Bedford challenged the Trade Descriptions Act with the name Better Than New. Alan and I jokingly referred to it as Better Than Nothing.

Dave owned a better-than-new Ford Transit Bedford van

which he used to run his own part-time removal business. Unlike Mick, our star porter, Dave's knowledge of antiques and objets d'art was sketchy. (Better Than New rarely displayed items of pre-1950 vintage.) This might not have mattered had he not prided himself on possessing what he liked to call initiative ('by the bucketful, Charlie'). A splendid quality in times of crisis, but a double-edged sword at other times when it could take the form of enthusiastic overconfidence.

We learned this to our cost when David Fletcher, our meticulous cataloguer, asked Dave to clear the remaining contents from a house in St Albans. I had previously visited the property and noted, among the several items of little value, a high-quality Kashan rug worth between one and two thousand pounds. It lay on a modern but good quality Axminster. As the house had been empty for a while, both pieces would have benefitted from a quick hoover. Notwithstanding, the vendor was delighted when I told him what I thought he could get for the Kashan at auction – so was I at the prospect of a handy auction fee.

Dave duly cleared the house and beetled back to our Woburn saleroom where he started to unload and carry the items upstairs. David, pencil and pad in hand, carefully checked in each object as it arrived. When Dave cheerfully announced, 'All done' and turned to go back downstairs, David called him back.

'What about the rug?'

Dave pointed to the Axminster. 'Over there. Sorry David, it got a bit crumpled when I took it up.'

David frowned. 'No, not that lot, Dave. The Kashan. Where's the Kashan?'

'The what?'

'The oriental rug.'

'Oh, you mean that dirty old thing lying around on top of

this one? Wasn't any point in bringing it over here, so I dropped it off at Bedford Tidy Tip to save you the trouble.'

Pause.

David, with considerable restraint: 'How quickly can you get back to the tip, Dave?'

The answer was about thirty minutes, which was nowhere near quick enough. By the time the owner of Better Than New had leaped from his van and pleaded with the man operating the refuse crusher to switch the machine off – 'Just for a second, mate, so as I can see if the boss's carpet's still OK' – its indiscriminate maw had devoured the Kashan in the same greedy mouthful as a rusty pram, seven dirty and threadbare sheets from a hotel that had gone bust, a broken Parker Knoll armchair, hedge clippings, and sundry household knick-knacks dumped by a thief who had failed to find a buyer for them in the Dog and Duck the previous evening. The unfortunate Kashan met its end a prince among paupers.

Dave, an honest bloke, was mortified. He was not the only one. The path to hell may not be paved with good intentions, but the path to penury certainly is. As an embarrassed David explained what had happened to the would-be vendor of the rug, I was writing him a cheque for £1,000.

Dave is an optimist. Hoping for a miraculous return of the crushed Kashan, he made a point of calling in on Bedford Tidy Tip whenever he was passing. After a while, the operators got to know him and, perhaps touched by the story of his last misadventure, took to saving bits and pieces they thought might interest him. About once a fortnight, a few quid changed hands and the items were transferred to Better Than New or, occasionally, to the Downer Ross saleroom in Woburn.

That's how Dave turned up one day with a silver-plated

Victorian biscuit barrel, a Georgian chest of drawers with no feet and an early 20th-century rug of unknown origin. Would we mind if he put them in our next sale?

I checked the objects carefully. The biscuit barrel was worth, on a good day, about £50–£60. Yes, we'd take that. The chest of drawers would probably fetch even more – maybe £100?

'And what's that third thing you've brought, Dave?' I grinned.

'Come off it, Charlie. You know I'm an expert on rugs.'

'Since when, Dave?'

'Look, I almost got some bloke to take it off me for twenty quid, so it must be worth something.'

I agreed. Although I wasn't too sure of its provenance, I thought it'd fetch at least as much as the chest of drawers. It was worth a punt.

On the day of the sale, Dave stood beside the podium in his smart, bottle-green Downer Ross porter's pinafore and indicated the objects as I announced their lot number. When the biscuit barrel sold for £60, his face split into a broad grin. When the chest of drawers went for an unexpected £360, I thought he was going to explode with delight. Then came the rug.

During the viewing day I had noticed one or two knowledgeable-looking dealers examining the mysterious rug with interest. *Ah-ha*, I thought. *Maybe Dave's "must be worth something" was not so wide of the mark after all?* Accordingly, I presented it with as much flourish as I could muster and nodded towards Dave. Like a schoolboy showing off his prize homework, he lifted the piece in the air and declared proudly, 'Showing here, sir!'

During the auction that followed, Dave had what might be described as a "Gorgon moment". For those who were asleep during school Classics lessons, let me remind you: the

Gorgons were mythical sisters who turned to stone all who looked on them. When the bidding for the rug reached £300, Dave's fingers stopped twitching; at £500 he was scarcely able to turn his head to see who was still in; by £1,000 all he could do was blink; and when the hammer finally fell at an astonishing £2,700, he was completely rigid, petrified by shock. He remained statuesque for well over five minutes as the auction carried on around him.

We leave Dave recovering from the impact of Rug Saga Part II and drive the short distance to his Better Than New shop in Luton. Eager to attract customers into this eclectic emporium, he had employed an attractive young woman named Caroline.

Caroline was charming and polite as well as good-looking – indeed, she would have made the ideal salesperson if she had known the first thing about the antiques and bric-a-brac business. For example, the names Clarice Cliff and Susie Cooper, prominent English mid-20th-century ceramic artists and designers, rang some sort of bell in her head, but not the right one.

One day, a customer browsed the contents of the shop before asking, in all seriousness, whether they had any work by the aforementioned ceramicists. Caroline hesitated, looked thoughtful, and made an imaginative jump from Clarice Cliff to the Cliff whom she had seen starring in the musical *Summer Holiday*.

'All the records are out on the pavement,' she replied with a smile, pointing to the box of second-hand discs on a table outside the shop.

When Dave told me this story, I asked what his reaction had been. Had he given Caroline the sack?

'No way!' he exclaimed, adding with a grin, 'We all make mistakes, Charlie, don't we?'

Too true, Dave. Too true.

One of the widely recognised delights of the auction process is the possibility, no matter how remote, that an object will fetch far, far more than either the vendor or the auctioneer anticipated. It underpins the success of the many popular TV antiques programmes. For instance, the 2012 *Antiques Road Trip* programme, in which a china elephant I bought for £8.00 sold at auction for £2,700 (see Chapter Fifteen), still attracts thousands of YouTube viewers.

Downer Ross used to conduct its own, small-scale (and untelevised!) antiques roadshow in towns and villages around Woburn. Following a bit of advance publicity, we set up stall in a suitable space and invited people to bring articles or photographs of articles for us to comment upon (where we could) and offer an estimated value. I sometimes surprised myself by how much I was able to deduce about an item I had never seen before. Decades of working in the antiques business had taught me far more than I could ever have learned from formal instruction: my school history teacher, who persuaded me to drop the subject before O-Level, would be astounded to learn that I can now recite the names of all the British monarchs from James I (and, confusingly, VI) to Charles III, with the dates of their reigns, though I still can't compete with Gilbert's famous Major General and reel off "the fights historical/From Marathon to Waterloo, in order categorical."

We are in the small Anglo-Saxon town of Newport Pagnell. Standing at a junction of the Roman Watling Street (A5) and the Grand Union Canal, it boasts a notable Georgian iron bridge which is still open to traffic. It was once the principal home of Aston Martin motor cars, too, and is still where Britain's only remaining vellum workshop operates. At the time of this Downer Ross Roadshow (c.1988), this proudly independent-minded little place, yet to be subsumed within the city of Milton Keynes, is an ideal venue.

It's a grey November day and I am seated beside Alan at a deal table in the chilly town hall, trying to look enthusiastic. Apart from a beautiful Sèvres porcelain dish, brought in by the wife of the manager of the local Barclays Bank, we have seen little of interest. I look at my watch, shuffle the papers in front of me and stifle a yawn.

'Time to go, Alan?'

As I am speaking, the door at the far end of the hall opens and a short, middle-aged man in a grubby raincoat walks in.

'Not yet, old boy. Another punter.'

I sigh and greet the new arrival with as much grace as I can muster. Pleasantries over, he takes out a poorly focussed and creased Polaroid photograph of a bureau bookcase and hands it to me.

'A dealer's offered me a thousand pounds for it,' he says in a voice that belies the raincoat. 'Should I accept?'

The camera might not lie, but it rarely captures the whole truth. I explain that I could not possibly value the piece from a photograph. Might I call on him and see it for myself? He agrees and we arrange a time to meet the following day.

I have my doubts even before I enter the rather modest semi-detached 1930s house in Water Eaton, on the outskirts of Bletchley. A rusty and untaxed Ford Anglia is parked at the kerb and the uncut grass at the front of the house is strewn with rubbish. Recalling the contrast between his rainwear and his speaking voice, I deduce that Macman (as I now think of him) has, as the Victorians used to say, "fallen on hard times". Perhaps I can help?

Macman, now wearing a green cardigan with two buttons missing, greets me politely and shows me into the kitchen. Six standard slat-back chairs are arranged on either side of a plastic-topped table. Uninspired, I look around ... and there it is!

Oh crumpled Polaroid! Couldn't you have done better

than that? It's truly magnificent: a classic Georgian walnut bureau bookcase. Sure, the handles are missing and the mirrored doors are shot, but the body of the piece is near enough immaculate.

'You know, sir,' I say, choosing my words carefully, 'the offer you received from that dealer was – how shall I put it? – a bit light.'

'Hum, I thought it might be. So what shall I do?'

'You enter it for the next Downer Ross auction with a reserve price of five thousand pounds.'

'How much?!'

'Five thousand pounds – not a penny less!'

The paperwork was soon completed and Macman and I carefully loaded his precious piece of 18th-century craftsmanship on to the rack on top of my antique dealer's Volvo estate. Would he be attending the auction? I asked, eyeing the clapped-out Anglia. No, he did not think he (or his car?) could make it. In which case, I said I would call him as soon as the auction was over and, assuming the bureau made the reserve price, put his cheque in the post the next day.

Back at Woburn, we took the bureau upstairs, cleaned it up, photographed it, and featured it in the *Antiques Trade Gazette* and in our own catalogue. When you have been in the business as long as I have, you sometimes get a "feel" about a piece, and I had a feel about Macman's bureau.

I was not mistaken. It attracted a lot of interest during the viewing and when, on sale day, I opened the bidding at £1,000, a forest of hands shot into the air. The reserve of £5,000 flew by and we were soon up to £10,000. I couldn't wait to phone the vendor with the good news – he'd be able to get the Anglia back on the road!

At £20,000 the bidding began to slow a little before John Butterworth, a highly respected dealer with a large premises on the A5, entered the fray. His presence confirmed my suspicion that the bureau was indeed special. I finally brought my gavel down at £32,000 and the auction room burst into a round of applause. I thanked all those who had participated.

'You have made my day,' I went on. 'In fact, you have made someone else's, too. This charming bureau is worth more than the vendor's entire house!'

A discreet "ahem" from Evan drew my attention to a man seated in the front row whom I had not noticed before. He was wearing a mac, a rather grubby mac. Yes, Macman had somehow got the Anglia running and had been sitting in the front row all along! Any hard feelings he might have had regarding my comment about his house soon evaporated when I made out the cheque.

CHAPTER NINE

Che Sara Sara

My experience with schoolmasters (see Chapter Two) was not always a happy one. I am hesitant, therefore, at suggesting I have anything useful to teach anyone. However, there is one question I am frequently asked to which I can offer an answer with a degree of confidence: how should the uninitiated behave at an auction?

In response I present **C**harlie's **G**olden **R**ules (my initials being C.G.R. – Charles Graham Ross – I rather like acronyms) for auction virgins.

Rule One. Don't try to be too clever.

Go with the flow: if you jump in with an exaggeratedly high initial bid in order to secure an item, you may well be successful. On the other hand, like the naïve young man at a Finchley auction who paid £500 for a coal scuttle decorated with an amateur depiction of Adam and Eve before the Fall, you may well end up paying far more than is necessary or wise.

At the other end of the scale, don't leave your bidding to the last minute. Goodness knows how many times I have seen hands or paddles raised a second after the hammer has fallen. Too late! Sorry, but at an auction "sold!" means "sold", and a plaintive, even tearful, cry of "But I was bidding, sir!" falls on deaf ears. It has to, or the auction process becomes meaningless.

On the subject of hands and paddles, do try to be clear. I remember Anthony Butt, a well-known dealer invariably dressed in a pinstripe suit with a brightly coloured silk handkerchief in the breast pocket, approaching me before one of our Woburn auctions with an interest in a pleasant-looking 19th-century Chinese porcelain plate. (This was long before ancient Chinese objects of any sort attracted astronomical prices.) Anthony was known as a furniture specialist and, although he planned to attend the sale to bid for other items, he wished his bidding for the plate to be anonymous.

'Alright, so how do you want to do it?'

'Here's the plan, Charlie: while I still have my glasses on, I'm bidding. If I take them off, it means I'm no longer interested.'

I thought for a moment before agreeing. I made a note in my catalogue: *Lot 24. Chinese plate. Anthony. In 2nd row – glasses on = OK. Off = no bid.*

When Lot 24 came up, I started the bidding at £30. The plate had clearly attracted interest, and we were soon up to £50, then £100. I checked row two – yes, glasses still on.

Two other bidders remained in the chase with the furniture dealer, and the three of them pushed the price up to a handsome £200. Anthony, his face inscrutable behind tortoiseshell spectacles, remained motionless.

At £250, the bidder from London, who I knew had an interest in Oriental objets d'art, dropped out. That left just the short-sighted furniture man and a woman in a Chinese-style dress with gold embroidery.

On we went. £280 ... glasses firmly in place. £300 ... not even a twitch from row two. Finally, at £340, the embroidered dress dropped out. I brought the hammer down and wrote the name of the bespectacled purchaser in my book.

When the sale was over, Anthony came forward to collect the items he had bought. 'Wow!' I exclaimed, 'bet you didn't expect so much interest in that Chinese plate.'

'Ridiculous, Charlie,' he said. 'Whoever paid that sort of money must be mad.'

'Er, glasses? Remember what you said? On ... off?'

'What? Glasses?' The penny dropped. 'Oh bugger!'

Being an honest chap, Anthony duly paid for the plate. Sadly, he is no longer with us. His heirs, however, might be interested to know that the plate they inherited is now worth at least ten times what he paid for it – and probably ten times more than the value afforded it for probate purposes!

As a rider, I ought to mention what is known as a "commission bid". It's a practice that allows a bidder to remain anonymous by informing the auctioneer beforehand of the maximum price they are prepared to pay for a lot. They may, of course, get the item for a lower price if the bidding doesn't reach their maximum. But a quiet word of warning: I'm told it's possible for an unscrupulous auctioneer (surely an extinct species?) to "run" the bidding up to the commission bid in order to increase their percentage-based fee.

Finally, the advent of mobile phones and the internet has made anonymous bidding even easier, though the task of an auctioneer becomes considerably harder. Juggling simultaneous bids from the floor, down the phone and on screen takes a fair bit of concentration, even when the phone bids are being expertly handled by my wife, Sally.

Rule Two. Decide in advance the maximum you can afford and stick to it.

This advice goes back to Classical times: "caveat emptor" or "buyer beware", especially at auction. There's something about a saleroom – the crowded space, the competition, the sense of danger – that makes people do foolish things. Add a glass or two, as is usually the case at charity auctions, and the bidding can get ridiculous. £10,000 for a pair of theatre tickets that would have cost you £300 at the door – crazy! But people do it. And not just the super-rich, either, which is why I am sometimes tempted to interrupt to save people from themselves. Tempted, but only once have I actually done so.

I am conducting the auction at the Silverstone Grand Prix charity ball, held the evening before the race. It is a celeb-laden affair, headed by one of the biggest stars of them all: Beyoncé. The organisers have generously allocated me a table of six onto which I have invited a few close friends and family, including Stewart and his wife Lucy. Before the auction begins, my brother, who can be rather lively on occasion, wonders whether he might join in the auction "for a bit of fun". Foolishly, I agree – as long as he drops out before the bidding gets sky high.

The centrepiece of the auction is a very grand, gleaming motorbike – Harley-Davidson, I believe – with the fuel tank generously signed by Beyoncé herself. The marquee is filled with very, very wealthy people and the bidding soon rockets up to £100,000, then into orbit at £140,000.

'Anyone give me one hundred and fifty thousand pounds?' I call. To my horror, I see a familiar figure on our table smiling and waving vigorously. An image of my sister-in-law standing beside the road, begging bowl in hand and dressed in rags, flashes through my mind. I have to stop this.

'Stewart,' I cry, 'shut up!'

He does, thank God. 'It was only a bit of fun,' he assures me afterwards. 'I don't really like motorbikes, anyway.'

'Yes, but if ...' I left the sentence unfinished.

When we were young, my brother once rescued me from a bullying cousin. Many years later, it was nice to be able to rescue him in return.

Talk of bids and bidding brings me back to our Woburn saleroom. I had four personal connections with our landlord, Andrew Russell, 15th Duke of Bedford, who lives in Woburn Abbey. The first, and most tenuous, was because my physio mother treated the Duke's grandfather, as a private patient of course, after he had suffered a skiing accident. The highlight of these domiciliary activities was not her patient's swift recovery, nor his charming manner and interesting conversation, but when she was given a private viewing of the family's world-renowned collection paintings by Giovanni Antonio Canal (1697–1768) – no less than 24 in one room. Her waxing lyrical about the Duke of Bedford's breathtaking Canalettos became a long-standing family joke.

My next connection with the duke was paying the Downer Ross rent, not personally by tugging the forelock and handing over canvas bags of pennies, of course, but by relatively painless standing order. Connection three came when the TV programme *Antiques Road Trip* brought me to the Abbey to do a short insert on Mary, the "Flying Duchess" (1865–1937).

As I had singularly failed to do at school, I did my homework and was pleased to note that, as in my life, luck had played a major part in the rise of the Russell family. In 1506, the Dorset gentleman John Russell came to the attention of Henry VII when the King and Queen of Castile were shipwrecked in John's back garden. John and his wife, who had the good fortune to speak French and Spanish, acted as both escorts and interpreters for their unexpected guests. The rest, as far as the Russells are concerned, is history. Bearing this stroke of good family fortune in mind, I was fascinated rather than overawed by the Abbey and its famous inhabitants.

Mary Russell was not a Russell at all. She was the last of five children born to Sophie and the Venerable Walter Tribe, sometime Archdeacon of Lahore, India. Though her unusual life story has often been told (even on *Antiques Road Trip*), I feel it sufficiently interesting to merit a swift recap.

In 1888, she married Herbrand Russell in West Bengal. When his brother died of diabetes in 1893, Herbrand inherited his title and became the 11th Duke of Bedford. Mary enjoyed a flamboyant career as a suffragette, philanthropist, ornithologist, nurse, and pioneering advocate of jujutsu. She was honoured during World War I for founding hospitals and serving in them as a nurse, work she continued into the 1930s.

At the age of 63, now almost completely deaf from infuriatingly severe tinnitus (and spending her weekends in the unfortunately named Whispers, the Russell mansion in Sussex), the Duchess took up flying with the same gusto as she had shown in her other activities. After a number of record-breaking international flights, at the age of seventy-one she decided she had had enough. Taking off in a De Havilland Moth Major with insufficient fuel in the tank to get her back to land, she headed out over the North Sea. Parts of her plane were later washed up on the Suffolk coast.

The Duchess story introduced me to the Russell family motto, *Che Sara Sara* (Whatever will be will be), a phrase the intrepid Mary seems to have taken to heart. As the aphorism chimed quite well with my own career, it stuck in my mind. There it remained until one day a man entered the Woburn saleroom with a brass inlaid rosewood standish ("a stand for holding pens, ink, and other writing equipment" OED). Would I enter the unusual piece into the next sale, please? Of course, I replied, and when he had gone I examined the item more carefully. The wood was in excellent condition and the rosewood base was inlaid with a brass inscription. Good heavens! *Che Sara Sara.*

My first thought was probably the same as yours: stolen property. I recalled the man who had brought it in. No, not the criminal type. Anyway, I reasoned, surely no one trying to get rid of an item taken from the Abbey would bring it to a public sale room only yards from where they had stolen it?

Deciding the piece was genuine, I reckoned I knew the ideal purchaser. Connection three.

'Evan?'

'Yes, Charlie?'

'Could you make a call for me?'

'Of course. Who to?'

'The Abbey.'

'The building society?'

'No Evan, Woburn Abbey. Our landlord. And ask please to speak to His Grace personally.'

'Really?'

'Yes, really. I have something that I think might interest him.'

I showed Evan the engraved standish, explained the motto, and off Evan went to the phone. He came back five minutes later grinning like, well, not like a Cheshire cat because I can't imagine anyone less feline than Evan. Let's say he was grinning like a hyena. Yes, he reported, Andrew, the 15th Duke of Bedford, would almost certainly like to bid for the standish. What was more, he'd pop into the saleroom and take a look at it himself – just to be sure.

'You mean he doesn't trust you, Evan?'

'It's not me he doesn't trust, Charlie ...'

The Duke of Bedford, genial, polite and not in the slightest bit aloof, turned up that afternoon. After a quick chat, he inspected the standish and booked a telephone line to bid for it at the next sale. I told him that although the piece was attractive, it had no special merit to the ordinary collector and would probably go for around £250. He thanked me and said he could "probably manage that amount". On the other side of the room, Evan nodded sagely.

The day of the sale duly arrived and when Lot 46 came up – a "silver Victorian standish or inkwell inscribed *Che Sara Sara*" – I opened the bidding at £200. Evan, glued to the telephone, indicated that the duke was in. I asked for bids of £250. A solitary, soberly dressed figure at the back of the room quietly raised the palm of his hand. *Ah,* I thought, *we have a contest.*

'Three hundred pounds anyone?'

The duke, via Evan, entered the bidding. So did the man at the back. In fact, he was prepared to go higher. £350 ... £400 ... £450 ... up and up the bidding went. I glanced again at the unknown bidder. Not a hair out of place. With his dark suit, white shirt and burgundy tie he might be ... an undertaker? No. The suit was too well cut and the shirt too neatly ironed. He was more like a character from a novel by P.G. Wodehouse.

Evan brought me back to reality. 'It's against you, Your Grace,' he whispered into the phone. Judging by his tone, the aristocratic would-be purchaser was clearly agitated. But he was no quitter. £900 ... £950 ... £1,000! This was extraordinary. I eventually brought my hammer down at £1,600. The duke had won, and the gentleman at the back, looking somewhat crestfallen, slipped quietly from the room.

An excellent price, I thought. To my left, Evan thanked his caller for his perseverance and said the lot would be ready for collection the next day.

The following morning dawned bright and sunny, and I was delighted to find the duke in a similarly cheery mood after his bruising battle the previous afternoon. Having assured me that he'd have the payment cheque sent over straight away, he asked, 'Come on then, Charlie, what on earth were you playing at?'

I hadn't a clue what he was talking about. 'I'm sorry,' I muttered. 'It was rather a, well, a full price.'

'Full price? You're telling me it was! Did you know who I was bidding against?'

I confessed that I did not. I had never seen the smart gentleman at the back before. Moreover, client confidentiality meant he had no idea who he was bidding against, either.

The duke picked up the over-priced standish and smiled. 'It was my mother, Charlie!'

Though neither the duke nor I had known it, the Dowager Duchess Henrietta had seen the standish in our catalogue and had sent her butler (aptly named Roger – known in the family as RTB) to bid for it on her behalf. In the end, I suppose, it didn't matter too much – the standish had returned to its original owners.

And me? We had made a useful commission, of course. Nevertheless, I was far more pleased to have my "character from a novel by P.G. Wodehouse" proved correct. One doesn't get Jeeves in the saleroom every day.

Only once in my pre-TV apprenticeship years did I come across a genuine hidden bargain of the sort that keeps viewers tuning in, week after week, to programmes like *Antiques Roadshow, Bargain Hunt*, etc. Shortly after we moved to Oxfordshire, I was asked to carry out a probate valuation in a nearby village. Having no formal qualification ("RICS, failed" did not look good on my notepaper, so I left it off), I was delighted to be asked to do this. At the same time, it was quite a responsibility. I was OK with furniture, but still a bit thin on ceramics, paintings and objets d'art. Nevertheless, nothing ventured, etc, and armed with a sound memory and a fair nose for quality, I accepted the commission. If I weren't sure of the value of something, I could always ask an expert.

For the contents of the house, which had been left to Mrs Anthea Unsworth by her elderly mother, this was not necessary. The objects I was asked to value were the sort of thing I came across every day – 18th- and 19th-century furniture, attractive paintings by little-known artists, and an array of tasteful bits and pieces. I totted them up and took the list to my client. Was she sure this was all? I asked, pointing out that the Revenue could be a bit difficult if they learned of undeclared treasures.

She thought for a minute before suggesting, 'Well, there might be something else worth looking at, Charlie. Mummy once told me she had a rather precious painting in the bank. She left it there because she said it was too valuable to hang on the wall. I've no idea what it is – rubbish probably. I don't think Mummy knew much about these things.' I didn't admit that neither did I at the time.

We called the Buckingham branch of the National Westminster Bank and arranged for me to meet the manager in a couple of days' time. Having checked my ID, he took an enormous bunch of keys and led me downstairs into the vault. *Too valuable to hang on the wall ... ?* I doubted it. Probably yet another print of Constable's Haywain.

Inside the vault, the manager hunted around for a minute or two before coming forward with a brown paper parcel. Carefully, we untied the string and unwrapped it. *Hmm, good frame ... Nice picture, too ... A vase of flowers in a sort of French Impressionist style ...* I examined it more carefully. *Certainly an original oil and not a print. This is more interesting than I thought.* I looked for a signature. *Yes, there it is ... not easy to read. Begins with an "F" and seems to end with an "n" ... the rest is hard to make out.*

It was time to ask an expert.

I went back to my client and explained about the impressionist-looking picture. Was she prepared to pay for it to be taken to London for a valuation by Sotheby's?

'Good heavens, Charlie! You mean it might actually be worth something?'

'It might, Anthea, and it might not. But there's only one way to find out.'

It was all getting a little bit exciting.

I called Sotheby's, who said they were interested and would be pleased to value the picture for us. Good, but how to get it to them? I couldn't just bung it in the back of the car and drive it there, could I? Not if it was worth thousands. Next call, Securicor. No problem. However, as the painting was not insured when inside their armoured van, I drove behind it all the way to Bond Street to keep an eye on it. I'm not sure what I would have done if the van had been hijacked – definitely not try to stop the thieves with one of my infamous rugby tackles!

At Sotheby's I was met by Michel Strauss, head of the Impressionist and Modern Art Department. Off came the string and brown paper and out came his magnifying glass.

'Well, well, Mr Ross! Do you know what this is?'

I resisted the temptation to give the obvious answer and said that the painting appeared to me a genuine French Impressionist by someone with a name like Fagin.

'Right on one count, wrong on the other,' he replied. 'It is indeed the work of a distinguished French Impressionist. His name is Henri Fantin-Latour (1836–1904) who signed himself "Fantin".'

I recognised the name and for a fleeting moment thought how wonderful it would be to have the painting in the next Downer Ross sale. The idea did not last long.

'Would Sotheby's like to sell the painting for my client?' I asked. Silly question.

'Indeed we would, Mr Ross!'

'Good. I think you'll probably get more for it in Bond Street than I would in our Woburn saleroom.'

'In all likelihood, Mr Ross. Yes.'

We will never know how much I could have got for Henri Fantin-Latour's Vase of Flowers (c.1890), certainly not the £200,000 it fetched at Sotheby's. I attended the auction, and though I was delighted by the price (as was Anthea), I was less impressed by the dry-as-dust auctioneer. Downer Ross might not have had clientele able to pay 200 grand, but the experience would have been rather more entertaining.

Having resisted the temptation to keep the Fantin-Latour for auction at Downer Ross, a short while later I was a bit irritated by a client who failed to demonstrate even a smidgeon of even-handed generosity. It began during the afternoon of the viewing day before one of our Woburn sales when a member of the public came up and handed me £250 in cash. 'I found it,' he explained, 'in one of the drawers of that dressing table over there, and I thought I'd better hand it in.'

The sum was a lot more than the marble-topped pine table he indicated was worth, and I thanked him warmly for his honesty. As he walked away to continue his inspection of the rest of the items, I decided that virtue deserved some kind of reward and popped out to the nearest off-licence. I returned with a £10 bottle of champagne (yes, you could get Taittinger for ten pounds in those days) and handed it to him with the compliments of Downer Ross and the vendor. At first reluctant to accept it, he eventually did so with good grace.

I then phoned the owner of the dressing table. 'If you'd like to call round at the saleroom,' I explained, 'I have a pleasant surprise for you.'

The man – a rather sour-faced individual – came in fifteen minutes later.

'Yes, Mr Ross. What's this surprise then?'

I explained about the cash found in the drawer of his dressing table, how an honest man had handed it in, and how I had bought him a bottle of champagne as a thank-you. I then handed over the £240.

He looked at it and scowled. 'There was two hundred and fifty pounds of my money in that drawer. You had no right to spend it. I demand the lot, two hundred and fifty pounds.'

I took a tenner out of my wallet and gave it to him. The dressing table made £65 in the sale. It might have made more had the auctioneer been a little more enthusiastic about it.

One more Woburn story before the BBC comes knocking. As it was the moment when Downer Ross came closest to bankruptcy, in some ways it's the most exciting of all. Insolvency was avoided, thank goodness, thanks to the discretion and genius for extemporary explanation of our premier porter, the incomparable Mick Stevens. If the story needs a title, therefore, it must be Mick's Marvellous Moment.

When undertaking clearances of substantial properties heavily stocked with attractive furniture and objets d'art, we generally managed the viewing and auction on site. After a visit to the property, this is how Alan and I decided to handle the sale at Sherington Manor near Newport Pagnell.

As always, we made careful notes on all the items for sale and checked their authenticity. Yes, the precious collection of Biedermeier furniture was genuine, the fine Chinese porcelain was unchipped, and the paintings were signed by artists of repute. The only thing we did not pay much attention to was the geography of the manor itself. We should have.

The building had a fascinating history. Dating back to the Norman Conquest (1066), it was surrounded by a decorative moat fed by water from the nearby River Ousel. At some point in the Middle Ages, a new manor was built outside the moat, and in the 18th century the site of the first house was landscaped into a garden and orchard. The moat was left intact as a charming water feature.

Preoccupied with the house's spectacular contents, Alan and I gave no more than a cursory glance at the spacious grounds before we hired a large marquee in which to hold the auction. Conducting the sale in the garden meant we did not have to move the outdoor statuary, including a substantial stone bath said to date from Roman times.

Moat, bath ... Looking back, I can now see that water-related vocabulary was increasing ominously. Mick added to it by insisting that "Biedermeier" was pronounced "Bidet-Mire".

The preparations went ahead as planned. First, we listed all the items for sale in a glossy brochure, then assembled them in a large room at the bottom of the house from where they could easily be carried to and from the marquee. The timetable was the standard one for such occasions: two days for the public to view the contents of the sale, a day to set up the auction, auction day, and two days for the successful bidders to collect their purchases.

After we had set up the sale in the marquee, Evan agreed to stand guard that night to deter robbers. In case his presence alone was insufficient deterrence, he armed himself with a shotgun and truncheon! Fortunately, the night passed without incident.

The following day's sale was a considerable success. All the lots exceeded their reserve prices and a gentleman from London in a claret-coloured velvet suit – whom Evan and Mick, our loyal porters, dismissed as "a twanny with more money than brains" – outbid all rivals to pick up every stick of the Biedermeier. We drove away under lowering skies to toast our success in The White Hart. By the time we got home, it was raining quite hard.

It continued to rain all night. When I woke up in the morning, so did a farmer whose fields lay upstream of the Manor. To prevent the Ousel topping its banks and ruining his corn, he opened a sluice gate on his land. Down the normally slow-flowing stream hurtled a mini tsunami. It swamped the moat and overflowed into the garden, the marquee ... and the ground-floor room where we had moved the furniture for safe keeping. We arrived to find a longcase clock, 18th-century chairs and the precious Biedermeier furniture floating in about a foot of water.

There was no need to send out a dove in search of dry land, for the waters soon subsided. Nevertheless, the scene inside the furniture store was horrific. Panic stations! While the porters, including Mick, scraped, mopped and polished inside, outside Evan summoned the purchasers to the marquee and delivered an impromptu seminar on how best to transport and store the items they had bought the previous day. The key, he said, was to take their time. Some of his audience were a little sceptical and exchanged quizzical glances. Fortunately, the velvet-suited Mr Twanny was not one of them.

After about half an hour, with the crowd in the marquee growing restless, Mick looked out of the window and muttered, 'Come on Charlie. You've got to let them in now.'

I glanced at the Biedermeier. 'But we can't leave it like this!' I cried. 'You can still see the stains.'

Mick put a kindly hand on my shoulder. 'Don't worry, Charlie. I'll fix it.'

I shrugged and slipped out of the storeroom to help Evan. When I returned a couple of hours later, I found to my delighted surprise that the purchasers and their furniture had all gone. Mick stood alone in the middle of the room, grinning like a slice of Gouda cheese.

'Mick,' I gasped, 'how did you? I mean why didn't they ...?'

'Told you he had more money than brains, didn't I Charlie?'

'Who? You mean the gentleman who bought the Biedermeier?'

'Gentleman to you, Charlie. Twanny to me.'

I had to smile. 'So what happened, Mick?'

'In he comes, peers at the furniture he's bought and asks what the marks are. He hadn't noticed them before, he says.

'I'm all innocence. "Really sir?" I say.

'He frowns a bit, trying to look like Sherlock Holmes, and says they look like watermarks.

'So I congratulate him. "Well spotted, sir! That's just what they are. Watermarks. Proof that the article's genuine. Like on your notepaper."

'That threw him. He muttered about learning something new every day, took one more look at the stains, shrugged, and got his porters to carry the stuff off.'

'Mick,' I exclaimed, grasping him warmly by the hand, 'you're a genius! As long as he doesn't bring the stuff back.'

'No worries about that, Charlie. A bloke in a suit like that would never admit to being made a fool of by a porter.'

He was right. We never saw the Biedermeier – or Mr Twanny – ever again.

CHAPTER TEN

For I am a Pirate King!

I owe my wife Sally a huge debt of gratitude for almost half a century of selfless love, guidance and support in my various enterprises. She is my pilot in choppy waters – and puts me down if (when?) I get a bit bumptious! Equally important, she has insisted that too much rostrum, too many days spent scribbling notes on catalogues, makes for a less effective auctioneer. There is, she reminds me, another type of note that is equally if not more precious.

This strange, eventful history began with the other types of notes Sally was referring to: the crotchets and quavers of the tune I was born to, "Put another nickel in". It will probably end with music, too – something funereal, though that chapter has yet to be written! In the meantime, the story would be incomplete without a few words on the important part singing has played in my life. Are there staves and semibreves in my genes? Perhaps. My mother had a good ear, though she never sang or played an instrument. In his infancy my father had a serious ear infection that left him partially deaf, and at school never got beyond "progress with scales", for which he was awarded (inexplicably) a prize. There was definitely some music in his soul, however, for when not under the eagle eye of my mother he would give hilarious renditions of the Edwardian music hall ditty, "Tell me, pretty maiden," in which he sang both male and female parts. The song still features at Ross family gatherings, usually with me singing the opening line and Stewart the falsetto response, tunelessly. Uncle Mac was musical from the top of his head to the tips of his elegant fingers: he could sit down at the piano and, without a sheet of music, play any tune requested of him.

Music first enters most people's lives through some sort of electronic device. For several years this was denied to my brother and I because – even as I write this, I find it almost incredible – we had no mains electricity. Let me explain.

My mother, wishing to be thought posher than she really was, refused to live in a house with a pavement outside or a number on the door. The homes of those she aspired to emulate were not on city streets but set amid rolling acres. When an opportunity arose to rent a flat in the isolated and semi-abandoned Stoke House midway between Bletchley and Stoke Hammond she seized it with relish. What an address!

Mrs Marjorie Ross
Stoke House
Stoke Hammond, Bletchley
Buckinghamshire

With that at the head of a letter, she could be mistaken for genuine gentry.

Alas! Though the address was posh, the reality on the ground was not. Lack of mains sewage was the least of our difficulties: many houses in the country managed with cesspits. Lack of mains water and electricity were more of a problem. Water for the header tank in the roof was pumped from a well beneath the house. As the pump was electric and we had no mains electricity, that should have meant no water or labouring for hours on a massive hand pump. Whatever his faults, my father was immensely practical. Only he, I believe, could have harnessed the lawnmower to the water pump. Thereafter, to refill the tank, one simply had to start the lawnmower. Elementary.

Connecting to mains electricity was trickier. Stoke House lay midway between the areas served by East Midlands Electricity Board and West Midlands Electricity Board, and neither would go to the considerable expense of linking it to the National Grid. Between the wars, the difficulty was solved by installing a massive diesel generator and a long series of 12-volt batteries. The system had ceased to function before we moved in, obliging us to light our flat with candles and Tilly lamps, and heat it with Aladdin stoves and a coal fire.

After a few weeks in our residence of shabby gentility, our father was poking around in the extensive network of outhouses and stables when he came across an even older generator system. It was rusty and had no backup batteries, but with a little coaxing he got it to work. Miracle! The lights came on and the lawnmower could return to cutting grass. Unfortunately, the old generator ran on petrol – and petrol was expensive. Ever practical (and always short of money), my father came up with another of his extraordinary Heath-Robinson solutions. He found that the generator motor, when warmed up, would run on paraffin, which was much cheaper than petrol. He topped up the fuel tank with paraffin, filled the carburettor with petrol, and started the motor. Fingers crossed … It worked! By the time the petrol in the carburettor had been used up, the motor was sufficiently warm to continue running on paraffin.

Hey presto! The lights went on again! But not for long.

About a week later, the rusty petrol generator, forced into service after years of idleness and fed the wrong fuel, burst into flames and died. Back to Tilly lamps and candles.

The two electricity boards eventually settled their differences and we enjoyed the luxury of electric lights, kettles and other gadgets. Among the latter was a record player. It was one of those old-fashioned types that took a stack of vinyl records, 45s, EPs and LPs, on a spindle and dropped them one at a time onto the turntable. One of our first LPs was an original cast recording (Julie Andrews, Rex Harrison, Stanley Holloway, et al) of the musical *My Fair Lady*. I was smitten and sang along to the record – as well as the Beatles and other pop bands of the era – over and over again. When I came to audition for a part in the show, I didn't need the lyrics on paper. I knew all of them, for every part, off by heart.

At school I learned that I could sing and, more importantly, that I enjoyed it. I even mastered the Latin lyrics of the ridiculous school song (*Carmen Berkhamstediense*) which I can still sing today, if prompted. I joined the school choir as a tenor – straining a bit – and learned to relish the wonderful harmonies of magnificent choral works, such as Stanford's *Te Deum*, which we sang in the school chapel on Sundays.

In good public school (paradoxically, "public" = "private" in the UK) tradition, everything, even singing, was competitive. Every year an inter-house singing competition was held, first with the whole house of around 50–60 boys in unison, then a part-song for eight voices: two each of treble, alto, tenor and bass. There were silver cups for the winners of each competition. Our unison song was chosen by the house tutor; yes, the same man who punished me because my father had a puncture. He was a classical music aficionado whose choices could not have been further removed from the tastes of the press-ganged choir. Young men exalting in "Twist and Shout" did not take readily to Mozart's aria *Non più andrai* ("Say Goodbye Now to Pastime") from *The Marriage of Figaro*. I was much happier taking the tenor line in the part-song "Come away, fellow sailors" from Purcell's *Dido and Aeneas*. I am still able to warble my way through it at family gatherings.

After I left school, for a few years my singing was largely limited to bawdy ballads in the rugby clubhouse. These were certainly not sung in Latin and rarely in tune. As for the lyrics, they are probably best left in the tankards from which they sprang. (Nevertheless, I am rather proud of the fact that after all these years I can still recall some of them, albeit through a beer glass, darkly!)

My sole venture towards something more salubrious came in 1971 when, goodness knows why, I auditioned for the part of Freddy Eynsford-Hill in Bletchley Operatic's production of *My Fair Lady*. Clambering onto the stage in a drafty hall and accompanied by an enthusiastic pianist in fingerless gloves, I made what I hoped was a reasonable stab at "On the Street Where You Live".

'I have often walked down this street before,' I sang, imagining myself strolling down Bletchley High Street in straw boater, past Irons the shoe shop where my mother bought my Clarks sandals ... 'But the pavement always stayed beneath my feet before,' I continued, now looking in the window of Neal's the toy shop where we bought track and rolling stock for our model railway ... 'All at once am I several stories high,' as the familiar façade of W.S. Johnson and Co the estate agent came into view –

'That's sufficient Charlie, thank you. I think that's enough for us to make up our minds.'

I made my way quickly out of the hall. *Thank goodness that's over!* I thought, certain that I would not get the part. Had another person wanted it, I am sure I would not have done. But no one else came forward and the director phoned to say how delighted he was to offer it to me. Freddy Eynsford-Hill was mine!

I panicked. I had never sung on stage before. Besides, I knew no one else in the company. It was all too much for a young man whose confidence was only just beginning to recover from the battering it had taken after fifteen rounds with an A-Level Bruiser, and I turned the part down in a fit of anticipated stage fright. Those of you who have seen me auctioning, chatting away merrily in front of the TV cameras, and on stage at the Oxford Playhouse may find this hard to credit. All I can say is that confidence is a delicate flower that needs to be carefully nurtured before it blooms. Besides, appearances can be deceptive.

Sally has a good soprano voice and an arresting presence on stage. In 1984, now Charlotte and Oliver were old enough to be left with a babysitter, she auditioned for the Oxford Operatic Society and was immediately accepted. Shortly afterwards she stepped onto the stage of the Oxford Playhouse as a member of the chorus in Jerome Kern and Oscar Hammerstein's ground-breaking *Show Boat* (1927). Impressed by the music I had heard around the house for weeks, ("Ol' Man River" is the best-known number – not sung by Sally, I hasten to add), I was eager to see how the company handled it. I was seriously impressed. Sally, of course, was excellent, but so too were the staging and the singing of Jim McClue and Mary Hedges. The urge to sing came flooding back, together with the remembered excitement of acting. Thanks to my experience on the rostrum, the crippling stage fright that had made me turn down Freddy Eynsford-Hill 13 years earlier had all but evaporated, and following a successful audition I was accepted into the company. As the society's ratio of women to men was about 5:1, I suspect the bar for admittance was pretty low!

1. Safe in the arms of my big brother, 1951.

2. My father and I on Climping Beach, 1951.

3. Stewart (the large one) and I in Berkhamsted School uniform, c.1964.

4. First taste of greasepaint: as Ford in a 1967 school production of *The Merry Wives of Windsor*.

5. Berkhamsted School 1st X1 (cricket), 1967. CGR second from left in the front row.

6.   Buckingham Rugby Club Exiles XV, 1983. I am third from left in the back row.

7.   Astonishingly, the Richard Ellis team, featuring a remarkably svelte CGR (the tall one in the back row), won the 1972 RICS 7-a-side Rugby Tournament.

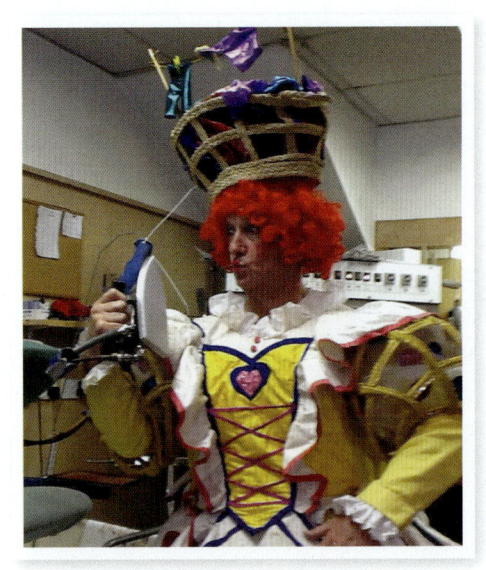

8. Panto time: Widow Wonkey in Bicester Choral & Operatic Society's production of *The Magic Lamp*, 2012.

9. As Professor Higgins in Bicester Choral & Operatic Society's *My Fair Lady*, with son Olly as Freddy Eynsford-Hill & Kerry Ayers as Eliza Doolittle, 2005.

10. Auctioneer in disguise: playing Fagin in Bicester Choral & Operatic Society's production of *Oliver!*, 2004.

11. The Pirate King carries off his loot in Oxford Operatic Society's *The Pirates of Penzance*, 1998.

12. At a charity event, 1985. The charismatic lady on the right needs no introduction.

13. The Downer Ross auction room, Woburn. I was never sure whether the first-floor location gave the impression of grandeur or poverty.

14. The magnificent Anglo-Indian Partner's Desk at the heart of my Nottingham adventure.

15 and 16.
A George Bullock sofa, bought for £190, painstakingly restored, and eventually sold for £32,000 – before and after restoration.

17. The sumptuous collection of Canalettos at Woburn Abbey. My mother always secretly hoped that she might be given one as a tip for her physiotherapy services!

18. Liz Zettl, famous in the office for her unorthodox operation of the space bar, and subsequently a character in the BBC drama *The Sixth Commandment*, 2023.

19. Any further bids? Auctioneering in the Woburn saleroom, c.1990.

20. Tea for two: Christina Trevanion and I enjoying *Antiques Road Trip* in the Scottish Highlands, 2014.

21. Doing my best James Bond impersonation, with Honor Blackman in *Celebrity Antiques Road Trip*, 2012.

22. Doing time for *Bargain Hunt*, 2019.

23. The Staffordshire Indian Elephant that carried me into the national newspapers. *Antiques Road Trip*, 2012.

24. James Braxton and I about to brave the freezing North Sea for *Antiques Road Trip*, 2012.

25. Our youthful Executive Producer, Paul Tucker, Caroline Quentin, Terry Wogan and me relaxing during the filming of an episode of *Celebrity Antiques Road Trip*.

26. The locking mechanism on an Armada Chest of the type that got me into hot water during my first appearance on *Antiques Roadshow*.

27. I learned more history on *Antiques Road Trip* than I ever did at school. On a visit to Northampton, I learned of the remarkable career of Walter Tull, pioneering Afro-Caribbean footballer and soldier.

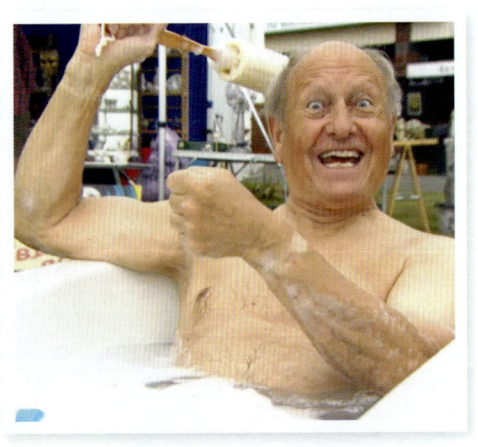

28. The things I do for Bargain Hunt … bubble bath, 2023.

29. With Jarvis Cocker (right), Bez (left), Rowetta Idah (second left) and Candida Doyle (second right) during the "cheating" episode of *Bargain Hunt*, 2018.

30. High kicks from the *Bargain Hunt* red and blue teams, with Philip Serrell and Thomas Forrester – and my MCC braces in the centre!

31. The *Bargain Hunt* rocker!

32. With fellow rock stars Philip Serrell, Charles Hanson and James Braxton in the Saga Entertainment Christmas Song, 2017.

33. My normal footwear is rather conservative but for The Honeypot Children's Charity auction I was most elegantly shod, courtesy of Sir Elton John!

34. Panting for Sands (Stillbirth and Neonatal Death Charity) during the Great North Run, September 2013.

35. Enjoying myself hugely as the "View from the Boundary" guest on *Test Match Special*, 2022 (Radio 5 Sports Extra).

36. Serious business with the Lord's Taverners Cricket XI: Chris Tarrant and I discuss tactics.

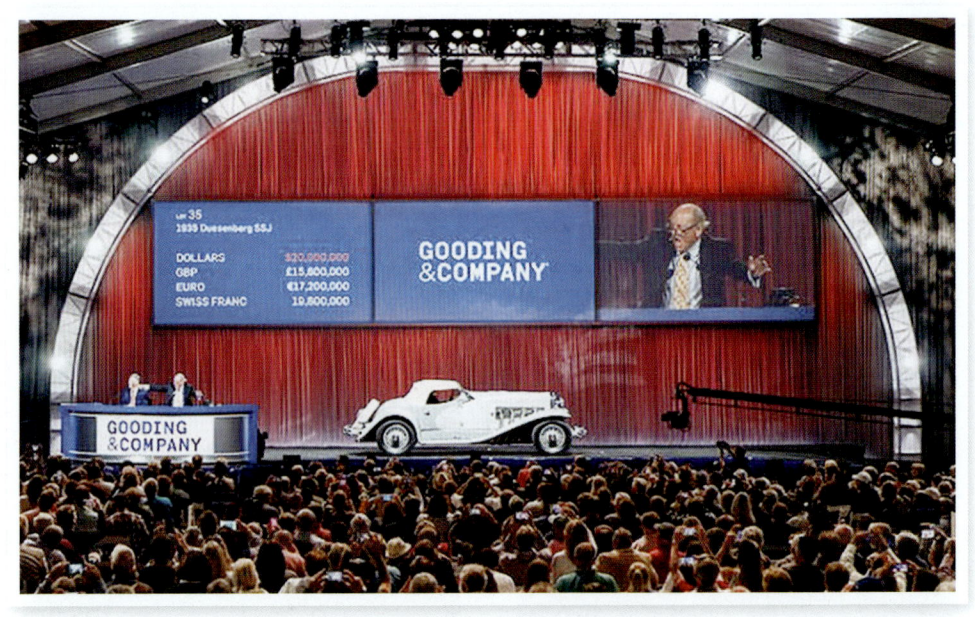

37. Going, going … knocking down a rare Duesenberg at a Gooding & Company auction, Pebble Beach 2018. It fetched a record $22M.

38. Covid or not, the show must go on: at the Gooding & Company auction in Hampton Court, 2020.

39. Offscreen and onto stage with Philip Serrell and Christina Trevanion on our *Antiques and a Little Bit of Nonsense* theatre tour, 2023–2024.

40. No Gooding & Company auction would be complete without a starring performance from Sally, aka Lady Ross!

41. Sally and I on our wedding day, July 30 1977.

42. The Ross/Macdonald Clan, Easter 2024. Charlotte, Max, Finn, Gemma, Grandpa, Ana, Granny, Olly and Zac.

My first part was in the chorus of Franz Lehár's popular operetta *The Merry Widow* (1905). The show opens with a ball celebrating the birthday of the Grand Duke of Pontevedro, a made-up tinpot Balkan principality. As the chorus of distinguished ladies and gentlemen raise their champagne glasses to drink a toast, all is glamour and sophistication – until one of them, carried away by the excitement of the occasion, drops his glass. With a resounding tinkle it shatters into a thousand pieces across the stage. Not an auspicious start, Ross, C! (Memo for future productions: never use real glass on stage.)

Fortunately, the incident was forgiven as "one of those things" and I was not thrown out of the society. The forgiveness of the director, David Hebden, went to my head. *Obviously, he doesn't mind if things go a bit off-script*, I thought. *It might even be amusing.* With this in mind, for the final performance on Saturday night I arranged for the chorus' glasses to be filled not with sparkling water but with the real thing, champagne. Never had the ladies and gentlemen at the ball sung with such unalloyed gusto, never had the Grand Duke been toasted with such swagger, and never had the scheming Baron Zeta, the subject of the toast, manoeuvred around the stage with such oily obsequiousness! This time David was not amused. If I did anything like that again, he warned me, I'd never feature in another Oxford Operatic production.

I learned my lesson and promised to stick to the rules in future. As a consequence, during the 1980s I was invited back to play a number of leading roles. The first was Curly in Rodgers and Hammerstein's evergreen musical *Oklahoma!* (1943), a curious role for someone whose hair was receding fast. Then came the Pirate King in Gilbert and Sullivan's operetta *The Pirates of Penzance* (1879). As on the rostrum, I attacked the role with vigour; so much vigour, in fact, that standing aloof and singing full blast "It is a glorious thing/ To be a Pirate King" I split my black leather buccaneer trousers right down the middle to reveal an equally buccaneering pair of red underpants! Having thighs built for long jump rather than fashion always was a problem.

From a pantomime villain to a real one: my next major part was Bill Sykes in Lionel Bart's *Oliver!* (1960). Although it's a hammy role that doesn't require much singing (even Stewart played it once!), there's plenty of scope for spectacular Victorian melodrama, and neither Nancy nor I held anything back during her gruesome murder scene. We generally earned a respectful hush from the audience – but not on the Wednesday evening of the week's run, when the theatre was filled with members of the Oxfordshire Women's Institute who had been allocated cut-price tickets.

The hapless Nancy cowered in a corner as I declared in my best thug voice, 'It's a dark night, my dear, but it's light enough to do what I've got to do!' With that, I lunged towards her and raised my cudgel. She let out a piercing scream and put out an arm to protect herself. In vain. Down came the cudgel. Again she screamed, even more terrifyingly this time. Never had there been such drama! I bashed at her until, with a final whimper, the poor girl subsided to the floor and died.

For a few seconds, total silence. Then a shrill, angry voice from the third row of the stalls cried out, 'Get off her, you big bully!' and the entire theatre collapsed into peals of laughter. Thus ended my first and last attempt at tragedy.

After that, it was back to more light-hearted roles until, finally, I was given the part I had dreamed of playing since listening to Rex Harrison on our ancient LP all those years ago: Professor Higgins in *My Fair Lady*. Like Bill Sykes, the Professor's singing isn't up to much – Harrison managed it without really singing at all. Nevertheless, I soon learned that it's very difficult to play the part without Harrison's definitive, if unkind, performance at the back of one's mind. With the help of the directors, on each of the three occasions I took the role I did try to do something a bit different. I wanted my Higgins to be more likeable than the man presented by Harrison, who in real life was apparently a bit of a cad. I hope I'm not like that. Being a sentimentalist at heart, I believe it's possible for a bachelor professor of phonetics to fall in love with a flower girl, isn't it?

I also turned out for the local Bicester Choral & Operatic Society, enjoying a number of leading roles in shows such as *The Gondoliers*, *Me and My Girl*, and *The Merry Widow*. At one stage Sally and I co-directed a production of *The Mikado*. As I was frequently absent on auction duty, I'm not sure we divided the task very fairly. In the end that didn't matter too much: Sally is a better director than me!

I knew that my stage days were numbered when, during a production of *Die Fledermaus* in Bicester I forgot my words. I was playing Frosh, a non-singing role that required nothing but an ability to appear drunk. The part suited me, and the situation, perfectly. Jennie Candy, a close friend of ours, was prompting from the orchestra pit some distance away, and I couldn't hear a word she was saying. In desperation, I staggered to the front of the stage, raised a hand to my ear and shouted, 'Shpeak up! I can't hear a word you're shaying!'

It got a laugh and afterwards unknowing members of the audience commented on what an amusing new emendation the director had made to the text. I knew better. The writing was on the wall, not in the script.

Sadly, and perhaps fortunately, I am now too busy with *Bargain Hunt* and auctions here there and everywhere to have time for rehearsals and week-long runs of shows, and the curtain has fallen on my chequered stage career. In any case, I doubt I could remember any of the words nowadays. That's the joy of performing on the rostrum – no script!

My singing was not reserved solely for the stage. As well as turning out for the Oxford Operatic Society, Sally belonged to a small choral group that gave well-attended concerts every year. I joined them as an acceptable baritone and participated in a wide range of performances, including Handel's *Israel in Egypt* and Allegri's *Miserere*. The singing was hugely enjoyable, although, as the title of Allegri's piece suggests, there was little scope for jolly japes.

Shortly afterwards, Sally brought together some of the same people (including her husband) to form the Phoenix Singers, and the concerts continued with works such as Handel's *Messiah* and *Dixit Dominus*, Mozart's *Mass in C Major*, and Bach's *Magnificat*. Again, no place for "Tell-me-pretty-maiden-type" singing. This was, if I am honest, a bit of a relief. Sometimes it's pleasant to relax as an anonymous member of a chorus rather than as the one in the spotlight out front.

Finally, a chapter on the part music has played in my life would not be complete without a mention of the uber-talented Jeff Clarke, founder and artistic director of the unique Opera della Luna company (ODL). For a time, lacking a base from which to operate, ODL used the building behind our back door, originally refurbished for my mother, as its headquarters. Though neither Sally nor I are good enough to sing for Jeff, who employs only top professionals for his memorable takes on favourite works such as *HMS Pinafore*, *Orpheus in the Underworld* and *Die Fledermaus*, Sally joined the company board and assists in a multitude of administrative roles. I attend as many shows as I can, sitting near the front and roaring with laughter at the work of a man who, like me, sees no reason why humour and artistic quality should not mix.

CHAPTER ELEVEN

Elyot's Nose

Before I went into television and had to start watching how I dressed and behaved in public, my life as an auctioneer and occasional antiques dealer was punctuated by unconventional, often amusing occurrences. Several of these involved my friend and neighbour Elyot Tett. He's a gentle, genial man, notable for his delightful Belgian wife Christine, his business acumen, and his remarkable nose. I don't mean he sports a Cyrano de Bergerac-like hooter. Elyot's spectacular nose is metaphorical, an invisible organ of such sensitivity that it can sniff out a bargain where others see nothing at all or, at best, mere dross.

I was in awe of this nose. Indeed, it was seeing the organ in action that finally persuaded me that dealing was not really my metier. I didn't have the instinctive feel for a bargain, a sixth sense that somewhere, over the horizon, loomed a profit. Somewhere over my horizon, there always loomed a prophet, an Old Testament type with a long white beard who pointed at me and said, 'Charlie Ross, get on the stage!' I didn't, but the rostrum came pretty close. Looking back, it was in some ways better: alone before the footlights, I was always the Macbeth or Hamlet. Not even a superstar like Leonardo DiCaprio is always centre stage. Nevertheless, if I had my time again, I would probably aim for the Royal Academy of Dramatic Art rather than the Royal Institution of Chartered Surveyors.

Furthermore, and I say this not out of false humility but as a matter of fact: I was a bit too soft-hearted to be a really successful dealer. At the back of my mind I was only too aware that one man's profit is another's loss; consequently, perhaps as a result of having witnessed the losses suffered by my unfortunate, wholly unbusinesslike father, I felt a bit too much sympathy for the loser. My nature, I realise, is not sufficiently red in tooth and claw for pure business.

Nothing illustrates the mystical power of Elyot's nose better than what Conan Doyle would have called "The Adventure of the Anglo-Indian Partner's Desk". It is also an example of the 1980s antiques carousel in full swing.

'Fancy a trip to Nottingham, Charlie?'

My first reaction was that I was too busy. My second was that an opportunity to watch the nose at work was too good to miss. I might learn something, too.

'Oh alright, Elyot, Neal's is it?'

'Of course!'

Neal's was one of Elyot's favourite auction rooms. He'd seen some interesting pieces in the catalogue of an upcoming sale and wanted to be there to take advantage of any bargains that might come up – and enjoy a hearty, old-fashioned breakfast while he was at it.

In the presence of our watchful wives, Christine and Sally, Elyot and I go easy at breakfast time, making do with toast, thinly spread with butter or some ghastly substitute, and topped off with a teaspoonful of marmalade. But the Nottingham trip was an opportunity to break the rules. Elyot knew a little café …

We started early and were starving by the time we drew up outside Hollies Diner on the outskirts of the former capital of industrial lace making.

'Two full English, please.'

'One egg or two?'

'Two, please.'

'Hash browns or black pudding?'

'Go on! Spoil us – both!'

Feeling a little guilty, we sat down and waited for the treat to arrive. When it did, we could hardly believe our eyes. We had been expecting eggs, bacon, beans, mushrooms, tomatoes, fried bread, hash browns, and black pudding – and they all duly arrived. What we hadn't expected was to find them floating, literally floating, like flotsam on a cholesterol-laden ocean of grease.

Elyot looked up and sighed. 'Serves us right, I suppose.'

I agreed. 'Haven't exactly gone easy on the Castrol, have they?'

We ate what we were able to salvage, paid up and left for Neal's saleroom feeling two stones heavier. I have been back to Nottingham on several occasions since the greasy feast, but never returned to Hollies. Not so Elyot. On every visit, he confesses, he could not resist calling in at Hollies for one of their artery-clogging, sinful but utterly unforgettable full English breakfasts.

The Neal's catalogue was packed with choice items. Elyot quickly flicked through before scanning the room, nose a-twitch. Suddenly, like a hound catching a scent, he was off in the direction of a magnificent Anglo-Indian desk. It was a partner's desk, meaning one large enough for two people (the partners) to sit facing each other across it, each with their own drawers, small cupboards, etc set into the body of the piece.

Anglo-Indian was the term given to furniture and other items, mostly hand-made and of extremely fine quality, constructed in India for the British colonial market. The most popular materials were ebony, teak or camphor wood, often beautifully carved and inlaid with semi-precious stone, ivory or even, in some cases, bone. Items made for the Indian Army were frequently bound with brass for added strength. The heftier pieces needed elephants to transport them. Since there was no shortage of elephants in India at the time, this didn't matter too much.

The desk Elyot had his eye (and nose) on had arrived in Nottingham by ship and lorry, not elephant. It was made from the finest jet-black ebony, probably sourced from the Coromandel Coast of south-east India, intricately carved and very heavy – had it slipped overboard on its voyage from India it would have been lost for ever: on account of its density, ebony is the only wood that doesn't float. This desk, then, was something special. Even I, no expert on either ebony or Anglo-Indian furniture, could tell that.

The Neal's catalogue had put an estimated "come and buy" price on the desk of £500–£700. Elyot reckoned this was too low and he was prepared to go higher, maybe up to £1,000. 'That should secure it,' he suggested. I wasn't so sure. Nor was I sure that he was being realistic in his ceiling of £1,000. In case you have a picture in mind of Christine and Elyot doing the family accounts facing each other on either side of a whopping great Bible-black desk, I need to point out that Elyot had no intention of actually using it. As a dealer, he was sure to have in mind someone ready to take the desk off his hands at a profit after he had secured it at a reasonable price. So when he mooted £1,000 for the item, I guessed he had a client lined up who was prepared to pay him rather more.

The room gradually filled up with dealers, owners of

antiques shops and members of the public looking for good furniture at a knock-down price. The latter were disappointed as every lot sold for well over the price suggested in the catalogue. I looked at Elyot. 'Going well,' I whispered.

'Too bloody well, Charlie!' he hissed back, looking a little tense.

The bidding for the desk started at a paltry £300. As this was beneath Elyot's contempt, he kept his paddle by his side until the price hit £500. After that, the price rose steadily to the £1,000 ceiling Elyot had set himself. Would he drop out? No way! £1,200 came and went. So did £2,000, with Elyot still in. Unusually for someone normally calm and level-headed, he was having a bout of what is known in the trade as "dealer's urge". I blamed the Hollies breakfast.

As I watched, I noticed how Elyot was casting determined glances to his right. I looked across to Richard Green, a well-known and likeable dealer from the Leicester area, raising his paddle in sync with Elyot's. This was it – a tournament, a fight to the death between two big beasts of the auction circuit. One by one the other warriors fell by the wayside, leaving Elyot and Richard to battle it out. No two Arthurian knights fought with greater bravado over a dusky maiden than did those doughty dealers over a dusky desk. Blow for blow, thrust by thrust, higher and higher until, finally, Richard threw down his sword and surrendered the field to Elyot. The price of victory? £5,400, roughly five times the limit he had announced before the sale began.

I was astounded. I knew Elyot had a nose for a bargain – but five times his ceiling price? Surely, for once in his life, Elyot had got it wrong. Oh ye of little faith! By the end of the day, he had sold the desk on to a friend for £10,000. His profit paid for the petrol and the full English breakfast on the way up, with a substantial sum left over for a rainy day. Although, with a nose like Elyot's, there never were any rainy days. Well, there was one when for a while the clouds looked ominously heavy: The Adventure of the Anglo-Indian Partner's Desk, Part II.

Two years have passed. One sunny morning, the friend who had bought the ebony masterpiece came into Elyot's antiques shop in Chiswick and announced that his wife had taken against the desk, calling it a depressing, lugubrious great thing. Would Elyot sell it for him?

Of course he would. He put it in his shop on a sale-or-return basis with a price tag of £15,000 – the original purchase price of £10,000 for the friend with the discontented wife, and £5,000 to split 50/50 between himself and the vendor. Those were heady days indeed for the antiques market, a sort of South Sea Bubble or dot-com escalation that was bound to collapse one day. But that day in 1985 was not it. Shortly after the desk had been put on display, a dealer from Fulham Road came in and inspected it.

'I have a client who I'm pretty sure would love this piece, Elyot,' he said. 'May I borrow it for a couple of days?'

The two men knew each other well and Elyot had complete trust in the Fulham man's integrity. The prospective purchaser left and came back with a couple of elephantine porters. As the desk was disappearing out of the door, Elyot called, 'Take care of it! And remember, fifteen is the lowest I can go.'

'Right-o!' came the reply. 'Fifteen it is.'

The desk disappeared, the door shut, and Elyot crossed his fingers. To his delight, that evening the Fulham man phoned to say his client had seen the desk and said he'd buy it. 'Thanks so much, Elyot,' he concluded. 'I'll drop the cheque off in the morning.'

'Sorry, but I'm away tomorrow. Would you be good enough to drop it through the letter box?'

'Of course. 'Bye Elyot – and many thanks.'

'My pleasure. 'Bye,'

Except it was not Elyot's pleasure. When he picked up the envelope from the doormat two days later, he saw to his dismay that the cheque was made out for £1,500. He got on the phone immediately and explained to the Fulham dealer in no uncertain terms that he wanted the full £15,000, not a 10% deposit.

Silence.

'Can you hear me? I'd like the full amount, please, not just the deposit.

It turned out that the man from Fulham, failing to read the label on the desk carefully, had taken Elyot's fifteen to mean fifteen hundred, not fifteen thousand. No wonder he thought he had a bargain. Elyot was now faced with the prospect of either making a personal loss of £8,500 or explaining to his friend that he had sold the desk for £1,500, a loss on his purchase price of £8,500. Eight thousand plus pounds was enough to test any friendship and Elyot was seriously worried.

Fortunately, the man from Fulham was an honest fellow. He admitted his mistake and said he'd do what he could to get the desk back. You get some idea of how the chain of escalating profit worked in the antiques business when I tell you that by the time he tracked down the desk, it had changed hands three times. You also get an insight into the essential honesty and reasonableness of people working in the trade when I tell you that, once the error had been explained, every one of those dealers returned the money they had taken, and the desk found its way back to Elyot's shop unharmed. The whole episode had cost him a few sleepless nights but no cash. The nose was still intact.

As you may have gathered by now, Elyot Tett and his nose were (and still are) a bit of a legend in the antiques world. Part of his secret was keeping ahead of the game. Take George Bullock, for example.

In the early 19th century, the skilled cabinet maker George Bullock was commissioned to supply the furniture and furnishings for Great Tew Park in Banbury, Oxfordshire. He used native English woods, most commonly oak, inlaid with holly, ebony and brass. The delightful works always sold well, though until 1985 it was not particularly sought after. In that year, the estate changed hands and a lot of Goerge Bullock furniture was put up for auction. As interest mounted, so did prices, and George Bullock became very collectable. The "second Chippendale" some were calling him. Elyot's nose began to twitch.

It twitched still more vigorously when, walking past The Old Cinema antiques emporium in Chiswick High Road, he spotted a very tatty-looking sofa on the pavement outside. Superficially tatty, maybe, but the noble wood, the intricate inlay ... surely it couldn't be a Bullock? Not after the dealer who had it up for sale had got it for under £200? However, the master craftsman didn't sign his work and his distinguishing marks were not easily recognised, so one couldn't be sure. With an asking price of £190, Elyot considered it worth a punt.

He went to work straight away. First stop London's Victoria and Albert Museum where he found an archive of Bullock patterns and tracings. Yes, the tatty old sofa that he had bought for £190 was indeed by George Bullock. Elyot is an admirer of fine work in its own right, not simply as a way of earning a living. His house is full of lovely furniture accumulated over the years because he likes it too much to sell. The Bullock sofa could not just be patched up; it had to be restored to its original condition using the same materials applied with the same skills as when it was in the Bullock workshop. Though the work set Elyot back £5,000, when it was complete the sofa looked magnificent.

'Entering it for the next Downer Ross sale?' I asked hopefully.

'Kind of you to offer Charlie, but I think I can get a better price elsewhere.'

'Really? Better than Downer Ross? Where?'

'Sotheby's.'

I couldn't argue. Sally and I accompanied Elyot and Christine to the auction, all eager to see what a sofa bought for £190 could make. Answer: £32,000. Another startling victory for the Tett nose.

Elyot is good company – and an excellent source of information. His interest in George Bullock's work, for instance, fired a similar interest in me – with spectacular results. Somehow, by a sort of mystical osmosis, I acquired a bit of Elyot's nose.

Late one Friday afternoon in March 1987, a man came into our Woburn saleroom and asked for my advice. His aunt had died recently, leaving him her sole executor and beneficiary. Her house in Worthing, Sussex, needed to be cleared before sale. Should he get a local firm to take away the lot, paying him a nominal sum, or should he first see if there was anything of value? I suggested he go back to the house and take Polaroid photographs of the contents. Armed with these, I should be able to advise him of the next step.

The man's name, I had learned, was Anthony. He did as I suggested, popped down to Worthing at the weekend and returned with a pocketful of photographs, some better than others. I examined them carefully with him. Kitchen – nothing. Dining room – nothing. Sitting room – noth ... Wait a minute!

'Anthony, what's that in the corner, near the TV?'

'Oh, it's some sort of coffee table thing. Falling to bits.'

'Falling to bits or not, it looks as if it might be a bit special.'

After we had been through the rest of the pictures, Anthony had made a list of six or seven items I suggested were worth preserving. I advised him to take a van down to Worthing and bring them back to the saleroom, and on no account to forget the "coffee table thing".

'You mean it might be worth something, Charlie?'

'If it is what I think it is, Anthony, I believe it might be worth quite a lot.'

Inspired by the prospect of unexpected riches, Anthony hired a van and was back in Woburn twenty-four hours later. As soon as he pulled up, I opened the door at the back of his van and jumped in. *Yes! I was right!* Thanks to Elyot's tuition, I could now recognise the distinctive hand of George Bullock, even when the piece in question was very much the worse for wear. One of the legs was held in place with a crude bracket but the inlay was unmistakeably that of the 19th-century master cabinet maker.

To make sure, I followed Elyot's example. Guided by Lucy Wood, a scholar who was writing a book on Bullock, I went to the archives of the Victoria and Albert Museum and scanned through the tracings of the craftsman's inlay designs. No single one matched that of Anthony's piece, but the likeness was unmistakeable. A "Sofa Table in the manner of George Bullock" featured prominently in our next catalogue. It attracted a fair bit of interest and I sold it for £31,000. Not on a par with Elyot's sofa, but only a smidgeon off. Anthony was, of course, delighted to find that his aunt's coffee table thing was worth almost as much as her house!

Every Boxing Day evening, when our families are settled peacefully before the television and the level in the Glenmorangie bottle is nearer the bottom than the top, Stewart and I enjoy a game of online roulette. He spreads his bets between 4, 7, 28 and 29; I go all out on 32. Occasionally, very occasionally, one or other of us strikes lucky on the first or second roll, leaving them substantially in profit. Then follows a long discussion. To keep going in the belief that one is on a winning streak and therefore likely to make even more (and have more fun which, in our case, is the prime purpose of the game), or pull out while one is ahead? The latter is known in Ross households as "doing an Overland" or simply "Overlanding". Let me explain.

Over the years I conducted a fair amount of business with John Overland, a successful antiques dealer from Olney, Bedfordshire. We had become good friends and trusted each other implicitly. It came as no surprise, therefore, to receive a phone call from him one day asking for my advice. To his happy surprise, his quote of £2,000 for clearing a local house had been accepted and he was now in possession of what appeared to be a rather fine piece of furniture: a six-drawer mahogany library table with an unusual extra wide drawer for plans and maps. (A little extra detail for antiques connoisseurs: its four legs were "reeded" in the style favoured by Gillows, the furniture makers established in the 18th century by the Lancastrian craftsman Robert Gillow.) It was difficult to put a precise date on the piece, but John and I reckoned it was late George III/Regency, ie around 1815, the date of the Battle of Waterloo.

On receiving John's phone call, I drove over to take a close look at his acquisition.

'So, Charlie, what do you think it's worth?' John asked.

'It'd probably fetch a few thousand,' I ventured. 'You could always try.'

John smiled. 'Try? You mean put it in one of your auctions?'

'Why not? Nothing ventured …'

After a bit more chat and a cup of tea, John agreed to let me take the table away for entry in the next Downer Ross catalogue. I assured him we'd make it a special feature. On arriving home, Sally and I unloaded the table and locked it in the garage. That evening, guess who called in for a drink? Yes, Elyot Tett, the man with the remarkable bargain nose.

'Picked up a nice piece today,' I said casually as I poured him a glass of Hook Norton. 'It's going in our next sale.' Out of client confidentiality, I did not mention John's name.

The nose twitched. 'What is it, Charlie?'

'A George III library table. Good nick, too.'

'Where is it?'

'In the garage. Want to take a look?'

The nose was moving into overdrive. 'You don't mind?'

'Of course not.'

Off we went to the garage. The moment Elyot saw the table, his nose began a St Vitus dance.

'Charlie, I've got the perfect client for something like this,' he said, trying to suppress his excitement. 'May I borrow it for twenty-four hours?'

I hesitated. In the end, I decided it could do no harm as long as Elyot had the table fully insured and promised to return it the following day. True to his word, he brought the piece back on time. I was not surprised by what came next.

'Do you think your client would be open to an offer, Charlie?'

I said that I thought not, but as an agent I was duty bound to pass on any offer. At the same time, I explained how I would also remind the client that as the table had already aroused serious interest, they would be well advised to keep it in the auction. Who knew how high the price might go? Elyot said this sounded fair enough.

The following Monday I took the table to Woburn and paid for an illustrated, fully detailed advertisement for it in the *Antiques Trade Gazette*, the trade's leading newspaper. Sensing something special, we placed the table in the most prominent position in the saleroom. Tension was mounting.

That evening, Elyot phoned with his offer. He had shown the table to Archie Hobsbawm, an up-market London dealer, and between them they would be prepared to pay £7,000 for it. As John Overland had bought the table as part of a job lot for £2,000, Elyot's offer represented a considerable profit. And yet ... I knew that Elyot and his friend would be expecting to make a profit when they sold the table on. I called John and told him of the offer.

'How much, Charlie?'

'Seven thousand pounds.'

'Hmm ... Well done. So what should I do?'

Tricky. Caught between two friends, I answered as honestly as I could. 'I'm not really sure, John.'

After a pause, John said he was tempted but would have a chat with his wife and let me know their decision in the morning. The conversation was obviously difficult because he did not call back in the morning. Nor the day after that. Eventually, he phoned to say that he and his wife had talked the matter over at great length and decided to leave the table in the auction to "test the market". I said I thought it was a wise decision.

On the first viewing day the table attracted a lot of attention from dealers from all over southern England. John and his wife had been right: it looked as if the table might well fetch more than the £7,000 offered by Elyot and Archie Hobsbawm. Behind the scenes, the astute duo had come to this conclusion, too. No sooner had I got home that evening than the phone rang.

'Evening Charlie. Elyot here.'

'Surprise, surprise!'

'Why?'

'That Georgian library table is attracting a lot of interest from all over the place.'

'I know. That's why Archie and I want to up our bid.'

'Yes?'

'To ten thousand pounds. And in cash, too, if your client would prefer it that way.'

'But the table's already in the auction, Elyot. It's in the catalogue.'

'That's OK. If our offer's accepted, you can leave it there and we'll adjust the reserve accordingly.'

Blimey! I thought. *They really do want that table, don't they?* I finished the conversation with Elyot and called John to inform him of the revised bid. This was his roulette moment: his number had come up; should he pull out with a handsome profit or keep going in the hope that his luck would continue. He and his wife talked the matter over and decided to play safe.

'Cash, you said, Charlie?'

'Yes, if you want it that way. But be careful. You know the Revenue …'

'Don't worry, I'm a fully registered tax-paying company. No under-the-counter stuff. It's not worth it.'

'Of course.'

'So tell whoever it is, yes. We'll accept ten thousand pounds in cash.'

'Well done, John! That's a nifty eight grand!'

After I had put the phone down, I wondered whether, for once, Elyot's nose had let him down. I needn't have worried.

The sale day came and the saleroom filled with punters. For once, I was quite apprehensive about what would happen, especially as a couple of friends were involved. Elyot turned up and told me that he didn't mind whether the table sold or not as he and Archie had lined up a client willing to pay £14,000. John also came along to the auction to see what happened. He was a bit miffed to hear that the new estimate was £14,000–£16,000 but calmed down when I pointed out that, after commission had been deducted, the table would have to go for at least the reserve price for the new owner to make much of a profit at all.

'So the ten grand I got looks as if it was about right?' he concluded.

'Could well be,' I responded cautiously. I had seen too many auctions to agree wholeheartedly. Besides, when Elyot Tett was involved, one never knew what might happen.

About half an hour before the auction began, the saleroom phone rang. Donna, our secretary and administrator, answered and informed me that Gopha Prophet from Kapital-Markupp (pseudonyms, to be on the safe side) was sorry he wouldn't be able to get to the sale but could he have a quick word?

Damn! I was counting on Gopha to be one of the prime bidders for the Georgian table.

'Hello Gopha. Sorry you can't make it. We've got a piece here you might –'

'I know, Charlie. I know. That's why I'm calling. I'd like to leave a bid with you.'

'Excellent. How much?'

'Well, I think twenty-six thousand pounds should do it.'

I gulped. 'Sorry? Would you mind repeating that. I'd hate to get it wrong.'

'Twenty-six thousand pounds, Charlie.' With that, he ended the call.

So many thoughts rushed through my mind. If nobody else bids, do I sell it to Gopha for, say, £14,000 – the new reserve? The situation was further complicated by the arrival in the saleroom of John and Elyot, both eager to see what would happen. The former didn't want the price to go too high, lest he appear a fool to have accepted £10,000, and the latter wanted it to soar well over £10,000 to show how astute he had been.

Five minutes before the sale started, the phone rang

again. It was Gopha.

'Had another think about that table of yours, Charlie,' he began. My heart sank. Surely he wasn't calling to tell me he had found someone to attend the sale and therefore was withdrawing his bid?

No, he wasn't. 'Wouldn't want to lose it for the sake of a few pounds,' he continued, 'so make the bid twenty-eight thousand, please.'

The bid was what is known as a "commission bid". This means that the auctioneer has received a price on behalf of an absent bidder who will secure the lot at or below the commission price (allowing for saleroom extras) as long as no higher bid is received.

I started the bidding for the table at a modest £5,000. At this stage, John was pleased, Elyot dismayed. Their positions soon reversed when Dick Turpin – that really was his name – entered the bidding. Dick was a regular at my auctions. A tall man with a bushy moustache, he puffed continuously at a large briar pipe, shrouding the saleroom ceiling with thick clouds of Player's Medium smoke whenever he attended. The higher the bidding went, the more furiously he drew on his pipe. By the time I had called "£26,500 with me" (meaning someone – in this case Gopha Prophet from Kapital-Markupp – had entrusted me with a bid of that amount), the ceiling had all but disappeared.

I looked enquiringly at Dick. He shook his head, gave one last furious puff on his pipe, and disappeared down the stairs. The atmosphere cleared and I brought my gavel down. Sold!

For a man who had just made in a day as much as I made in six months, Elyot Tett looked remarkably calm. Not so John Overland, who had sold for £10,000 an item that hours later had fetched £26,500. To my surprise, he remained at the auction, bidding every now and again and finally buying Lot

536, the last one of the day. It was a shotgun.

'I didn't know you bought shotguns,' I said to him afterwards. 'What are you going to do with it?'

'Shoot myself,' he explained with a smile. He was joking, of course, but to this day I always think of him when my lucky number (32) comes up at roulette.

CHAPTER TWELVE

Flogging It!

If you've managed to read this far without nodding off or are just idly flicking through at a car boot sale, you are likely to know me – if at all – as the jolly bloke on TV. In which case, you are probably wondering, where's the *Bargain Hunt* stuff? Where are all the Very Famous People Charlie has met? Well, hang on! We'll get there in a page or two. You see, for most of my life the only TV that featured was the one in the corner of our sitting room (after the electricity had been installed, that is), and the sole well-known person I'd met was the actor David Tomlinson, and that was because I was asked to carry his wine order from the Bletchley off-licence to the boot of his Rolls-Royce parked outside. (We meet David again in Chapter Fourteen.)

The man whose house I entered on Winnington Road (next to The Bishops Avenue, aka "Billionaires Row") in 1984 was not particularly famous, but he was, like everyone else who lived in that corner of North London, enormously wealthy. He was "downsizing" – one could hardly upsize from a mansion like his – and a friend had recommended

Downer Ross as best able to get top prices for his surplus furniture, etc. As the vendor had more items of value than ever appeared in our Woburn saleroom, the auction was held within the house itself.

We produced a fine catalogue, ran eye-catching publicity, and the sale went very well – though not in the eyes of the vendor. Throughout the auction he sat on the sofa behind me squawking like a parrot 'That's too cheap!' every time I brought my gavel down. During my dealings with him over the previous few days I had already ascertained that he was – how shall I put it? – a little eccentric.

He rose late every morning and, leaving his splendid Rolls-Royce in the garage, drove a battered old Mini down to the shops 'for a shave'. The first time this happened, I was a little surprised to find him back on the sofa within fifteen minutes with stubble that looked as unkempt as when he had left. The second time, I found an excuse to inspect his beard more closely. He had certainly not gone for a shave. As he was explaining breathily that he expected a 'damned good price' for his set of dining chairs, I realised what he had sneaked out for: gin! The chairs, incidentally, fetched £14,000 – much too cheap of course!

Back in Woburn, I found myself dealing with a very different sort of client. One of these was Mrs Becket of Leighton Buzzard. I had a soft spot for Mrs Becket – let me explain why.

She lived in a modest 1950s house with her elderly, tight-fisted and, I came to realise, very unobservant husband. As far as I am aware, she did not go out to regular work but somehow managed on the meagre weekly allowance her husband gave her. I believe that from time to time she asked that it be increased, only to be refused. To make ends meet and to afford a few little luxuries for herself, she phoned the saleroom once or twice a year and asked Evan to pop round and collect an item or two and put it in the next sale. She made sure this was done when her husband was out.

This went on for two or three years without Mr Becket having a clue what was happening. By now, I don't think their house could have contained much more than a bed, dining table and fridge. Then one day – panic! Evan had just returned from collecting the latest haul and was arranging it for the next sale, when in rushed a flustered Mrs Becket.

'Play it cool, Charlie!' she gasped. 'Play it cool!'

Before I could ask what she meant, I saw her husband emerging at the top of the stairs. His wife and I held our breath as he made his way around the room, looking carefully at the lots. How on earth could I explain how objects from his house came to be there without betraying his wife? Round and round Mr Becket went, peering, lifting, examining – and eventually leaving without recognising a single thing!

In Yorkshire, they dismiss behaviour like this with a shrug of the shoulders and a wry "nowt so queer as folk". Down in Bedfordshire, Evan and I could only agree.

Freddie Unwin King was another slightly odd one. This small man, always neatly dressed in bow tie, waistcoat and Harris Tweed sports jacket, was one of our chief buyers. He purchased quality items for his upmarket clients, mainly in London's West End. Many of his best acquisitions went to Frank Partridge, the prominent art dealer operating out of the famous Partridge building opposite Sotheby's in New Bond Street. Downer Ross basked in this reflected glory.

His dapper appearance aside, Freddie had two trademark accessories. One was his smiling and comfortable-looking wife who accompanied him on his forays into the countryside. On viewing days, he gave her a handful of loose change to go off and find a cup of tea while he examined the lots. Accessory two was his immaculate Ford Cortina Estate.

He went to great lengths to keep this vehicle in mint condition, disengaging the odometer to ensure it would be low mileage when he came to sell it, and wrapping dusters round the foot pedals to minimise wear.

Evan and I found these antics rather amusing. Obviously, Freddie did not for, as was later confirmed, he had no sense whatsoever of the ridiculous.

This became clear when Freddie Unwin King finally decided that a dealer of his distinction needed something larger than a Ford Cortina Estate, no matter how well maintained, in which to transport his wife and his antiques. Accordingly, he purchased a handsome white Ford Transit van and had his name painted in large letters on the side. The first time it made a public appearance was at a large country house sale in Northamptonshire. After dropping his wife in a nearby town where she could find a cup of tea, Freddie drove up to the house, parked, and went inside to view the lots.

He returned after an hour and a half to find his van surrounded by a small crowd of fellow dealers, all laughing their heads off. He walked angrily up to them and asked what was so funny. One by one, without a word, they pointed at the sign painted so carefully, so tastefully, on the side of the van: FU KING Antiques. Freddie went home immediately and thereafter was never seen in anything but his spotless Ford Cortina Estate.

Freddie was a discreet, even secretive man who did not like to disclose who his clients were nor what his mark-up was when selling on items he had bought. Only once did he let the veil slip. At one of our sales, he paid £7,000 for a fine-quality Ormolu-mounted Victorian ornamental walnut centre table by Holland & Company. He wrote a cheque immediately and arranged for his couriers to take the table away. That, I assumed, would be that.

It wasn't. Two days later, I received a cheque from Frank

Partridge of New Bond Street for £7,700. The accompanying note explained that it was payment in full for the Holland & Co centre table. *Ah-ha, I thought, so that's who it went to. And only a 10% profit. How generous!* I immediately got on the phone to him.

'Good afternoon, Freddie. Charlie here. Just calling to say how modest of you to charge only a ten percent mark-up on that Holland & Co centre table.'

'What?'

'You remember. The lovely piece you bought at our sale last Thursday.'

'How do you know how much I sold it for?'

'Well, Frank Partridge has sent me a cheque for seven thousand seven hundred pounds!'

Pause while the news sinks in. Eventually: 'Blast! I must have slipped up somewhere, Charlie. Would you mind sending the cheque back to Mr Partridge?'

I did, that very afternoon.

Over the years, I have built up a small stock of quips that are generally well received by audiences. At charity auctions, for example, remarks like, 'Thank you – now you can go back to your drink,' or 'I'm tempted to say that I'd buy you a Scotch but that would be bribery, wouldn't it?' or 'Surely, if you've got twenty thousand pounds, you've got twenty-two thousand!' go down well, as long as they're delivered with a smile. As in other aspects of life, context is everything.

The same rule applies to more serious auctions. If the punters are on my side, I can slip in remarks like, 'Stop smiling – I haven't brought the hammer down yet!' or 'This is quite exciting – I feel two million dollars coming on!' or even 'Look at the car, sir, then look at me, and then put your hand in the air!' If the atmosphere in the room is suitably upbeat, I can even get away with mistakes involving huge sums of money: "2.4 million dollars – whoops, we're in

England – sorry … 2.4 million POUNDS!" (The context of this one is explained in Chapter Seventeen.)

I suppose the ability to come up with this sort of banter, inherited from my quick-witted father and honed over years of auctioneering, put me in good stead when, one morning, the saleroom phone rang and Evan answered it.

'Hang on a minute, please.' Covering the mouthpiece, 'Charlie, it's for you.'

'I'm busy. Who is it?'

Evan, still covering the mouthpiece, 'It's the Beeb.'

'Ah! Not that busy. Coming!' I went over to Evan and took the phone. 'Hello, Charlie Ross here. Sorry to keep you waiting …' And so it began.

The call was from a member of the team running the BBC's *Flog It!* programme. For those who haven't seen it, here's how the show worked.

Members of the public were invited to bring objects of unknown value before a panel of two or three experts who were filmed estimating what the items might fetch at auction. What viewers didn't know was that we, the experts, were backed up by a very knowledgeable team of off-screen valuers whose detailed advice we ignored at our peril! The owners were given the option of putting the experts to the test by having their possessions sold at a bona fide auction. This, too, was filmed, and included the auctioneer saying a few words about each lot before selling them.

The BBC was calling to ask whether Downer Ross would like their saleroom to be used for a *Flog It!* auction of items that had been valued in nearby Milton Keynes. I suppose there were some – people like Freddie Unwin King or my mother, perhaps? – who did not approve of the world of fine art and furniture being made the subject of popular television programmes. I was not one of their number. Downer Ross, at least the Ross bit of it, jumped at the chance for a bit of media publicity.

Working with Paul Martin, the programme's presenter, chatting about the lots and then selling them was good fun. Such good fun, in fact, that I asked whether I might do a bit more. Did they want another valuation expert? They might do, the producer said, but first they needed a proper screen test. Was I free to come to the next valuation day in Cambridge on Sunday? I had to be there by 8 am.

Without thinking, I accepted the offer. Not a wise move. The evening before I was booked to conduct the charity auction at the Formula 1 pre-Grand Prix ball at Stowe School, a boozy affair that started at 11 pm. Having done the auction, I unwound with a glass or two, jiggled away erratically in the disco for a while and was driven home by Sally. As I fell into bed around 3 am, I glanced at my diary. What was that? F-it 8 am – Oh no! 'F-it' was pretty appropriate: I'd managed to crash my media career before it had even started.

Miraculously, I hadn't. Sally hauled me out of bed at some ungodly hour and I made it to Cambridge by eight that morning.

'I'm here for the screen test.'

'What screen test, sir?'

'To see whether I can be an expert on *Flog It!*'

'Ah! So you're the other expert. You must be Charlie Ross. Come this way, please.'

Someone had blundered – or maybe (I flatter myself) the BBC had been so impressed by my Woburn performance that I didn't need a screen test after all. Whatever, I was taken straight in as a bleary-eyed, slightly hungover valuation expert. I dread to think what my fellow expert, the lovely Catherine Southon, thought of me at the time, especially when, first up, I was flummoxed by a pair of damaged Chinese vases. Knowing little about such things, I bluffed my way through ('They're chipped, of course, which reduces the value considerably') and valued them at between £60 and £80. They sold for £480! Catherine was kind enough not to pass judgement and we soon formed a friendship that has seen us working together on *Antiques Road Trip* and *Bargain Hunt* as well as *Flog It!*

Participating in *Flog It!* under the charming and efficient tutelage of Paul Martin was great fun, despite the hideous memories of school brought back by the word "flog". I enjoyed travelling round the country (though not always happy with the budget hostelries we were billeted in), meeting people from all walks of life, learning a great deal about what strange things were (or were not) worth, and making friends with other members of the expert panel. Charles Hanson, Christina Trevanion, Philip Serrell and I got on so well together that in 2022 we even put together a little touring show of our own, *Antiques and a Little Bit of Nonsense*.

At this juncture, the BBC and I made a mistake. Theirs was to ask me if I would like to join the *Antiques Roadshow* team, mine was to say yes. Both were understandable. On *Flog It!*, after learning on the hoof from countless auctions over many years, I showed some knowledge of the value of things, antique and otherwise. I also came across as a genial sort of chap whom audiences appeared to like. For my part, the chance to appear on one of the BBC's flagship evening programmes was too exciting to turn down.

The vibes were not good from the start. I met the team for dinner on the evening before filming was due to start. Several of them, notably Hugo Morley-Fletcher, Tim Wonnacott and Henry Sandham, were friendly and welcoming. I found the others harder work. A few snippets of conversation (NB how I was always "Charles", not "Charlie") will give you the picture:

'Sorry, Charles, but I've never heard of *Flog It!*. Is it some sort of daytime television?'

'Do people really watch television during the day?'

'What do you think of the latest find in Ulan Batur, Charles? Quite a remarkable piece for people who were, by all accounts, total barbarians.'

Q: 'An Oxford or Cambridge man, Charles?' '

A: 'Neither. Bletchley, midway between the two.'

'Oh, did you do your postgrad stint at Courtaulds?'

'You see, we're rather a close-knit group on this programme. A bit exclusive, I suppose. But I'm sure we'll find a place for you, eventually.'

It was clear even before filming that things were not going to be made easy for the new boy in the class. It is possible that some of the senior members – the prefects – were worried that someone who combined entertainment with expertise might take the show where they were not able to follow. Whatever, neither they nor I were willing to change.

This became only too obvious when valuation day dawned and I was asked to talk about my first items, a chart dating from the time of the Spanish Armada (1588) and a large, reinforced strongbox from about the same period. Before the cameras rolled, I chatted to the woman who had brought them along. We shared the same sense of humour and got on famously.

All is now ready. Unlike *Flog It!*, which generally had to manage on a bit of a shoestring, no expense is spared: three cameras, a bank of lights, and even a touch of make-up. Simon Shaw, the programme producer, hovers in the background to ensure all goes according to plan.

On comes the enormous strongbox, wheeled into view on a barrow normally used for moving sacks of grain. I turn to the woman who owns it and begin:

'Madam, how lovely to meet you. May I say what a magnificent chest you have.' She giggles, as do the camera crew and the makeup artists. The director does not.

'Cut! Charles, this is a serious programme, not Carry On Up the Roadshow.'

The scene was retaken without my little joke and on I stumbled. Whether deliberately or not, I was asked to discuss and value not a stick of furniture, about which I knew quite a lot. Instead, I was presented with an ill-assorted array of obscure objects that included a stuffed golden eagle, an apothecary's cabinet and a ventriloquist's dummy. I did my best.

After a few undistinguished appearances, I wrote to Simon suggesting that perhaps *Antiques Roadshow* wasn't really for me. He agreed, and I moved on to less serious programmes better suited to my wish to entertain as well as inform.

CHAPTER THIRTEEN

Road Trips

Working on STV's *Antiques Road Trip*, and its sister version *Celebrity Antiques Road Trip*, gave me some of the most enjoyable moments of my broadcasting career. For those not familiar with the hugely successful programme that started in 2010 and is still going strong (2024), *Antiques RT* works like this: two experienced auctioneers or dealers, generously dubbed "experts" by STV, drive around the countryside, stopping at antique shops and trying to pick up bargains with a fixed budget. In my day it was £200 each, though this has subsequently been increased. Their purchases are sold at auction; whoever makes the most profit, or (as was usual in my case) the least loss, is declared the winner of that episode.

To add a splash of colour and interest, not to mention unreliability and discomfort, the trips were made in a variety of "classic" cars. For filming purposes and for further panache (a touch of wind in the hair à la Grease, though sadly not for me), these had to be "convertibles" – ie open-topped. My fume-belching transports included a Triumph

Herald, a TR6, a Ford Consul, a Mini, and a Sunbeam Alpine. Oh the memories these cars brought back! I once owned a very ropey Sunbeam Alpine myself. The big ends were dodgy when I bought it, and after six months they sounded as if I had Ringo Starr in the sump. I managed to sell it by playing the radio full blast when I took the prospective buyer for a test drive. A double Beatles track – one from the engine and the other from the loudspeaker, did the trick, and he bought it! As for the STV Mini ... when we set out, I gave the director an anxious hour or two by recalling how my ever-practical father recommended fitting a condom over the distributor cap to keep the rain out in wet weather. Fortunately, it was dry for that trip. Classic indeed!

It was all great fun. The atmosphere was a bit like that of an old-fashioned amateur cricket match: my fellow competitors, including James Braxton, Charles Hanson and Thomas Forrester, all wanted to win, but certainly not at any cost. And none of us was grumpy when we lost. The dealers, auctioneers and their respective staff entered enthusiastically into the spirit of the programme.

STV, the company that makes *Antiques Road Trip* and *Celebrity Road Trip*, is a Scottish organisation. Not surprisingly, therefore, a good number of our trips were made around Scotland. After a sip of malt, I am inclined to claim that country as the land of my birth. This is, of course, nonsense: Aylesbury is 375 miles south of Edinburgh. Nevertheless, I have a kilt, support Scotland in sport, especially rugby, and my names – Charles Graham Ross – could hardly be more Scottish; nor could those of my brother, James Stewart Ross. The kilted names stretch back through my father, Graham Stewart Ross, my grandfather William Wallace Ross, to my great-grandfather William Stewart Ross (1844–1906), the last genuinely Scottish-born member of the family.

I am, I suppose, like many millions around the world,

best described as a sentimental Scot. I sob on the tragic battlefields of Culloden and Flodden and in the museum of the Black Watch Regiment. Stewart and I once went on a pilgrimage to the Ross family seat, Balnagown Castle, only to be turned away at the gate in dismay because the "laird" did not welcome visitors. And who was the laird? None other than Mohamed Al-Fayed. Despite Cairo being a fair bit further south than Aylesbury, he too had bought into the ranks of the sentimental Scot. My brother Stewart is also caught up in this bagpipery, having written several books on Scottish history (with blurbs that speak of his "unashamed Scottish roots"), and persuaded his wife that their children bear names from the Ross family catalogue: James, Katharine, Alexander and Eleanor.

The irresistible pull of the north on our family can be traced back to my great-grandfather, a distinguished poet, publisher and militant freethinker who wrote under the penname "Saladin". He was clearly a personality of great power. It was he who insisted that the Ross's link to the Stewarts, dating from a Ross–Stewart marriage in the early 19th century, means we are descended from Scotland's King James IV – "James of the Iron Belt". Saladin's forceful legacy explains why Uncle Mac's side of the family bear the surname Stewart-Ross. It also explains why Saladin's eldest son was known as "Chief" (of the clan) and not William, why my uncle was "Mac" not Wallace, and why I wear a kilt and support Scotland, not England, at rugby. It's my royal blood, you see.

So when STV's *Antiques Road Trip* took me north of the border, I felt as Bonnie Prince Charlie, the Young Pretender, had done when he landed on Scottish soil in 1745 to claim the throne, 'I have come home.'

Many of my Scottish *Antiques Road Trip* adventures and encounters stick in the memory. A dip in the icy North Sea with James Braxton in April is one, parading with penguins in Edinburgh Zoo is another, and being welcomed by the Macpherson-Grant family at their stunning Ballindalloch Castle is a third. Then there was the occasion when I chatted with Adrian Shine in The Loch Ness Exhibition Centre, Drumnadrochit, on the shores of the loch. This eccentric gentleman has devoted his life to exploring the largest expanse of inland water in the British Isles, even building his own tub-like mini-submarine from fibreglass in order to take a look below the surface. Had he found the legendary monster? No, but he did come across a World War II bomber on the bottom of the loch. He told me that his work had not been in vain: he might not have made startling discoveries in the field of natural history, but he had learned a great deal about what he tactfully called "human perception"!

For one of my Scottish jaunts, I managed to persuade the director to shelve the programme's insistence on an open-top car and allow me to swap a Morris 1000 for an old VW Campervan. The trip was made even more special when they allocated Christina Trevanion, described by someone online as "the hottest woman on TV", to be my competitor and fellow traveller. I can guess what some of you are thinking – but no. We are both happily married and the BBC booked separate rooms for us in local Holiday Inns. Except once.

'Wouldn't it be fun, Christina,' I casually suggested one evening as we were chugging through the Highlands, 'if we spent a night in the Campervan? Just for a laugh.'

I expected, at best, a polite, 'No thank you, Charlie.' To my surprise (and mounting panic) she said, 'OK. On condition that you go in the bottom bed and let me have the comfy one on top.'

I agreed. After a brief stop to pick up provisions, I pulled the van over into a small pine forest. In the gathering gloom, I disappeared behind a tree to change into my pyjamas while inside the van Christina pulled on a thick sweater (I wasn't looking – she told me afterwards) and clambered up to her eyrie beneath the stars. So far, so good.

In our quest for an authentic scouting experience, we had both chosen to ignore a crucial meteorological fact: at night, the temperature in the Scottish Highlands drops dramatically towards zero. I was starting to doze off when a plaintive voice from above whispered, 'Charlie, are you awake?'

'Yes. Just. You OK?'

'No, Charlie. I'm very, very cold!'

Hottest woman on TV? Hardly! Only one response was possible: I clambered out of bed, started the engine and headed for the nearest Holiday Inn. Fortunately, there was a night porter on duty to let us in. What he made of the late arrivals, an old man in his pyjamas and a young woman in a scarf and three sweaters, I'll never know. There was a clue, however, in his deadpan reply when I asked for two rooms: 'Of course, sir!'

An unexpected pleasure of *Bargain Hunt* was being educated. As I explained in Chapter Two, my years of formal education were not satisfactory. I ended up with a smidgeon of science and even less art, literature, history and geography. Years on the rostrum and in the saleroom filled in the yawning gaps in my art curriculum, while *Flog It!*, *Antiques Road Trip* and, later, *Bargain Hunt*, reduced the blanks in the other three disciplines. Having a fairly inquisitive mind, I couldn't visit a place without learning a little about its geography and history.

A couple of examples will suffice. Exploring the museum of the Black Watch Regiment, originally the 42nd Regiment of Foot, I was startled to find that it had been formed after the 1715 Jacobite Rebellion to keep my ancestors, the wild and lawless Ross clan of north-east Scotland, under control. Rosses lawless?? Never! Researching that episode of *Antiques Road Trip* alone involved crash courses in Jacobitism (incorporating a soupçon of Latin to understand where "Jacobus" comes from), British religious history, and what was right and wrong with the Stuarts (Scotland's "Stewarts", our ancestors). Incidentally, I also learned that no one really knows why the Watch was named "black".

I was even more surprised by what I learned on my *Road Trip* visit to Northampton. Being a keen supporter of the town's rugby and cricket clubs for many years, I thought I knew the town quite well. Wrong. I could find my way to the rugby club, cricket ground and railway station, and I knew the place had once been famous for making leather shoes. Trivia! My incidental STV history lesson taught me that in medieval times the town had hosted meetings of parliament – yes, Northampton is another Westminster – and in 1880 it returned the first avowedly atheist MP, Charles Bradlaugh. I checked him out. Gosh, a surprising family link: Bradlaugh was a co-warrior with my great-grandfather Saladin in the ranks of rebellious Victorian freethinkers. And previously I had thought the only links were on a golf course or on the cuffs of smart shirts ...

Northampton had not yet finished with me. When war broke out in 1914, professional players in the Northampton Town football team were urged to sign up. The first to do so was their prolific goal-scorer Walter Tull (1888–1918). Nothing remarkable in that, you may say. But hang on! Walter, described in one report as the "most brainy forward", was one of Britain's first professional footballers of Afro-Caribbean heritage – his grandfather had been a slave in Barbados. Respect and admiration for this remarkable man rose even higher when I learned that in 1917 he became a fully-fledged officer, the first from his background to be commissioned into the ranks of the regular British Army.

Tull died months before the war ended. In a further tragedy, a fire in the War Office destroyed the commendation recommending him for the Military Cross for an "act of exemplary gallantry".

All this fascinating history under my nose and I had no idea ... I'm not sure what this goes to show other than learning is so much easier when we're enjoying ourselves. At least, I find it so!

It's time to hit the road again. Charles Hanson and I climb into our ancient motor and head for King's Lynn on another *Road Trip* adventure. My geography's coming on in leaps and bounds, and I can now place the ancient fishing port at the top right-hand corner of East Anglia. Another trip takes us west, into Wales. Here we call in at Dylan Thomas's writing hut perched above the boathouse where the Welsh poet lived with his family during the last years of his life. As it overlooks the "sloeblack, slow, black, crowblack, fishingboatbobbing sea" of the Tâf Estuary, I can't help but pick up a bit of Eng Lit. After geography comes history: a trip takes us to Portsmouth and the tary decks of HMS Victory. By the time we leave, I understand that there's a bit more to Trafalgar Square than protest meetings and cup winners falling into fountains. We have fun en route, too. I am pelted in the stocks, sing with a Welsh Male Voice Choir, play Scrooge wearing a nightshirt in Leeds Castle, and race a lawnmower. When all these trips are over, I am a good deal more learned than when I set out.

This quick resume makes it all sound like a jolly romp. Some of it certainly is, but not all. Take the King's Lynn visit, for instance. As we enter East Anglia, we are near the ancient port in terms of distance, but way off in terms of time. The reason for the delay is our vehicle. Charles and I are at the wheel, alternately, of a 1967 (Vietnam War, Summer of Love, "Lucy in the Sky with Diamonds") Ford Corsair. It looks like a pirate ship on its side and drives like one except less reliably. During the fifteen days of filming it breaks down five times. After one of these malfunctions, we decide to leave the car where it is and each make our own way to the elusive King's Lynn. Charles sets off on foot; I stay where I am with the cameraman, raise my thumb and smile. It works. After five minutes, a newly qualified doctor on her day off pulls up and asks if we needed assistance. 'I stopped,' she explains later, 'because you didn't look like normal hitch-hikers – not at all threatening!'

Ah, the joys of old age!

In we pile, me, the cameraman and equipment, and once again we set off for King's Lynn. We haven't gone more than a few hundred yards before we come across a man at the roadside behaving very strangely. He's standing with one foot in the road, waving his arms in imitation of a swimmer doing butterfly. The doctor puts her foot down.

'No!' I yell. 'Sorry, but please stop! It's Charles!'

The doctor takes her foot off the accelerator. 'Charles who?'

'Charles Hanson. He's making a programme with me.'

'Then why's he impersonating a windmill?'

'I don't know. He's probably never hitched a lift before and doesn't know how to do it.'

I am right. Once Charles is safely on board and sitting beside the cameraman, I explain to the doctor who we are and what we are doing.

'Hasn't the car been serviced, Charlie?'

'Probably not. Can't afford it.'

'I thought you TV lot were millionaires?'

I laugh, she laughs, and we all spend a very pleasant afternoon preparing for the next day's shooting.

While we were enjoying ourselves, the Corsair was recovered from the roadside and repaired. We soon learned that "repaired" is a subjective term. Given a temporary lease of life would be more accurate. As Charles and I made a grand entry into King's Lynn Market Square the next day, the Corsair decided it had gone far enough and conked out. We pressed the starter until the battery was almost flat, to no avail. Not a spark of life beneath the bonnet.

The director phoned for assistance while Charles and I wondered what to do.

'How about a game of cricket, Charles?'

'What, here?'

'Why not? There's a bat and ball in the boot, and there's plenty of space between the payment meter and the exit barrier. The BMW over there can be the wicket keeper.'

'Are you sure?'

'Of course! The owner won't mind.'

For those of you who don't know the game of cricket, the "wicket keeper" is the baseball equivalent of the "catcher" – in other words, the person who takes the ball if the batter misses it. I was the batter in our impromptu Market Square test match. Charles was the bowler ("pitcher" in baseball terms). To my alarm, he was a better bowler than I had bargained for. Ball after ball went whistling past my bat and came perilously close to the side of the immaculate BMW wicketkeeper. Fearing for her paintwork, the car's owner, a stout lady in a Barbour jacket, abandoned her shopping and strode angrily onto the wicket.

'I'm calling the police!' she announced as another of Charles's rocket deliveries zoomed past her head and hurried past the pristine panelling of her car.

'Please don't! We're only having a little fun ...'

'Too late, vandals! They're on their way.'

Three members of the local constabulary turned up a minute or so later and told us in no uncertain terms to move on. 'As far as I'm concerned, sir, it don't matter if you're filming the Ti–bloody–tanic, but you're not doing it in this car park.'

In vain we explained that nothing would please us more than to move on, but our car ...

'You'll have to push it, sir!'

Charles and I looked each other. As his reckless bowling had very nearly ruined the lady's car, I argued, I would sit in the Corsair and he would push. No, he retorted, if my batting had been any good, the BMW would have been in no danger whatsoever. Reluctantly, I acknowledged there was some logic in his argument. He got into the driving seat. I pulled up my sleeves and got ready to push.

'Ready?'

'Yes, Charlie. Wagons roll!'

After about ten metres of heaving and cursing, I gave up. Police arrest, I decided, was better than cardiac arrest. We swapped places and tried again. Same result. Although twenty metres from where it had started, the Corsair remained as dead as Latin. I got out and stood beside Charles.

'So what do we do, Hanson?'

Before either of us could say anything, a woman hurried out of Boots the Chemist crying, 'I had one of those things once. Bloody awful! But I do know how to get them started.'

We believed her. The knight in shining armour, who had announced herself as Denise, got behind the Corsair's wheel as Charles and I prepared to shove. Off we went, round and round the Market Square. To cheer ourselves as we pushed, Charles and I sang the Blondie number, 'Denise, Denise, I've got a crush on you!'

Eventually, after three or four circuits of the square, the Corsair spluttered into life and I collapsed to the ground in exhaustion. Charles did not join me. He had been chatting to Denise during the Great Push and learned of a much better antique shop than the one allocated to him by the director. When he said he had to see it, Denise offered to take him there. I hauled myself to my feet just in time to see him disappearing into the distance riding pillion on the back of Denise's moped.

That's not quite the end of the story. We duly spent £200 on antiques from our King's Lynn shops and watched eagerly as the items were auctioned. Thanks to an unexpectedly high bid for a rusty sword, mine fetched £310. Charles's goods, bought at the shop recommended by Denise, went for £185. Ancient Berber proverb (alleged): It is easier to rouse a corsair than sell a donkey.

Celebrity Antiques Road Trip (2011 onwards) works on the same basis as the regular programme, except the two contestants are celebrities, each assisted by an "expert". The celebrity contestants, often from the world of showbiz or sport, add programme appeal and are never shy in front of the camera. On the whole, they were enormous fun to work with.

Given my love of cricket (confirmed in the next chapter), you will not be surprised to learn that travelling around with David Gower (b.1957), the former England captain, leading TV commentator and general all-round superstar, was an unalloyed pleasure. For me, that is. David seemed to have a good time, though I find it hard to believe that he really enjoyed being cooped up all day with an elderly groupie whose only experience of the game at international level was sitting behind the boundary rope.

The unruliest celebrity was, without doubt, the irrepressible Irishman Terry Wogan. I worked against him rather than with him, for he was teamed up with Charles Hanson in competition with the actress Caroline Quentin, whom I assisted. Caroline and I worked well as a team, and we ended the day with a nifty selection of lots that we reckoned Terry and Charles would find it hard to beat.

We were right – but not before Terry had turned the saleroom into a madhouse. He started by suggesting the contestants, not the auctioneer, should sell the lots they had bought. No, said the series director firmly, that was not the way the programme worked.

'But this edition is the exception,' Terry declared, jumping onto the rostrum and starting to call out for bids. The director, unable to stop him, buried his head in his hands and the auction continued with each team taking it in turns with the gavel.

When we came to Team Wogan's final lot, I learned something else about Terry: he was extremely competitive. Charles and he were losing by a long way and all they had left to sell was a Chinese vase for which they had unwisely paid £120. They needed at least double that to win. Undaunted, Terry hoisted the vase in the air and, to the accompaniment of solid gold Irish blarney, paraded it around the room as if he were the showroom porter. 'Now this vase, I assure you, is no ordinary Chinese vase ...'

The punters smiled – some even laughed – and they all agreed with him. It was no ordinary Chinese vase. It was, in fact, a less than ordinary one, so much so that the bidding stopped at £30.

For a second, the man famous for being able to talk himself out of paper bag was lost for words. Then the answer came to him. If no one else would bid for this wonderful vase, he'd bid for it himself! £35, £40, £50 ... Finally, at £70, with the director on his knees begging him to stop, Terry dropped out. This brought the bidding to an abrupt halt, enabling Caroline and I to win the day.

I was fifteen when the film *Goldfinger* was released. Given my sheltered, all-male upbringing, I didn't get the double entendre in the name of the female aviator who played opposite James Bond. However, it didn't stop me being bowled over (as was Bond) by the attractiveness of Honor Blackman, the actor who played Pussy Galore with such memorable allure. Later, when it dawned on me that Pussy's allure was further enhanced by her naughty name, I wondered how on earth, in 1965, it managed to get past the censors. (In case the blue pencil struck, the studios had the flaccid "Kitty Galore" in reserve.) My favourite explanation is that before the film's release in the US, Honor was photographed at the London premiere standing beside Prince Philip. This gave newspaper caption-writers, aware of Philip's bachelor reputation, an unmissable opportunity: "The Prince and the Pussy". After that, now Pussy had royal approval, there could be no backtracking.

In 2012, STV called with a ridiculous question: would I like to do a *Celebrity Road Trip* with Honor Blackman and Britt Ekland? To be honest, I would have paid them for the opportunity rather than the other way round. I was slated to accompany the late, great Honor Blackman while Britt would travel with Charles Hanson. Perfect.

No, not quite perfect. What car would I be driving Pussy Galore around in? I asked. A rather embarrassed STV executive replied, 'Er, things are a bit tight at the moment, Charlie. Austerity and all that. We've lined up a Morris 1000.'

'A what??'

'A Morris 1000. Don't worry, it's in tip-top condition.'

'Hang on a moment, please ...'

Tip-top condition or not, I was not going to ferry Pussy Galore around the country in a district nurse's tuk-tuk. I put down the phone on STV and called Martin Chisholm, a vintage car specialist from the Cotswolds whom I had met in Pebble Beach.

'Good morning, Martin. How much would it cost to hire an Aston Martin DB5 for three days?'

'Depends what it's for, Charlie.'

I explained that it was for me to chauffeur Honor Blackman.

'Where would you like the Aston delivered?'

'Can you manage Cambridge?'

'Consider it done.'

'That's very good of you, Martin. But you still haven't told me what it'll cost.'

'Nothing at all. I couldn't possibly charge for you and Honor!'

And that's how I came to spend three happy days roaring around East Anglia with Honor Blackman. Though the Aston Martin was the same model as that used in the film by Sean Connery, I am no James Bond. However, my spritely 86-year-old passenger was still Pussy Galore – she had a real interest in antiques, too!

On the second evening, after a long day's filming, I asked Honor if she would like to have dinner with myself and the rest of the crew. She declined politely, saying she was rather tired and would have an early night. *Ah well, I might not look like Bond*, I thought, *but at least I can try and behave like him.* I asked the waiter to take a bottle of champagne up to Miss Blackman's room.

When Honor came down the following morning, she asked whether I had been responsible for the champagne. I said that I had.

'That was so kind of you, Charlie. I drank it while soaking in the bath.'

Of course. Once a Bond Girl, always a Bond Girl. I was sixty years too late!

CHAPTER FOURTEEN

Howzat!

For as long as I can remember, cricket has been my favourite sport. I am aware that this presents a problem for American readers for whom a great deal of what follows may as well be in hieroglyphs, unless they are scholars of ancient Egypt, of course. English readers will, I hope, allow me a few words of explanation.

The basic game of cricket is simple; its details and vocabulary are not.

The essence of cricket (for non-cricketers).

- One player, with his or her arm straight at the elbow, throws (it's called "bowling", not to be confused with rolling heavy balls in alleys) a small hard ball in an attempt to hit three pieces of wood stuck in the ground (the "wicket") at the further end of a twenty-two-yard strip of grass (the "pitch", not to be confused with a throw in baseball).

- A player of the opposite team (the "batter", not to be confused with the coating of a piece of fish in a fish and chip shop) tries to hit the ball (like a striker in baseball) with a willow "bat" (obviously) in an effort to stop it hitting the wicket.

- If the batter manages to hit the ball well enough, they can run twenty-two yards to the other end of the pitch. This, unimaginatively, is termed a "run".

- The eleven players in each team all have a go at batting (an "innings"), and the team with most runs wins the match. This can take up to five days, 11 am to 6.30 pm.

Simple ...

Now you understand the game, my transatlantic friends, I can proceed with the story of my cricketing life.

I like to think cricket is in my blood: I am told that my maternal grandfather, an ardent supporter of the Surrey County Cricket team, died one summer evening while seated in his potting shed listening to the day's cricket scores. When he heard that Surrey's innings had come to a close, his did too. Whether or not he played the game is immaterial. Cricket, like baseball, is a game of intricate statistics and is followed by many millions (it's India's national sport) who have never bowled a ball or wielded a bat.

I am not one of those. I have played, often, but never very well. My cricket career started with a flourish when I captained my school Under 15 team. Bowlers, like car drivers and thinkers, are either fast, medium or slow. In 1965 I was fast. I was a reasonable batter, too, featuring in the "middle order" – ie numbers 4, 5 or 6 in the batting order. The end-of-season report in the school magazine records that my standard way of hitting the ball (ie my favourite "shot") was the "hit to leg". (The "leg" side of the wicket is on the batter's left; their right side is "off"; stylish cricketers like Joe Root "drive" the ball on the off. For left-handed batters, the nomenclature is reversed.) It may not surprise you to learn that, despite the team's generally poor results, "morale was never low ... mainly due to his [ie my] cheerful disposition." As on the rostrum, so on the cricket field.

The smiles soon faded as my cricketing career, like the share index in a bear market, followed a depressingly downward curve. Having made a bit of a name for myself at junior level, aged sixteen I was selected for the school 1st XI as someone who batted and bowled with distinction. Wrong on both counts. I'm unsure what went wrong – lack of concentration or talent or (probably) a combination of both – but before long I was demoted to the 2nd XI. In my final year at school I was a common foot soldier in the 3rd XI, its third most effective bowler and seventh best batter.

Despite these setbacks, my passion for the game remained undimmed. For a few years I played for the Great Brickhill village team, with limited success until my last match. It was earmarked as a charity event to raise funds for the 15th-century (heavily restored) church of St Mary the Virgin. I approached a wealthy local (unrestored) virgin, Miss Jones, and asked her to sponsor me in the worthy cause. She knew little of the game and offered £1.00 for every run I scored. Remarkably, since my usual top score was in single figures, I made 71. The cheque Miss Jones happily handed over, worth £2,138.77 at 2024 prices, was sufficient for new prayer books all round with enough left over for a kettle in the vestry for the vicar.

From village cricket I graduated to club cricket with the Northampton Saints. At this level my bowling, considered fast at school, was regarded as nothing more than erratic medium pace, and I was thwacked all over the field. It was time to reconsider. Now the proud father of two lovely children, Charlotte and Olly, I no longer needed to prove my athleticism. Besides, my hairline was receding and I drove a Volvo. I therefore decided to leave the fast bowling to vigorous youngsters and act in accordance with my status in life: I would become a slow bowler, full of guile and craft.

Slow bowlers are "spinners", meaning they spin the ball with their fingers so that, after striking the pitch, it bounces off at an angle. With luck, the batter takes an almighty swipe and misses because the ball is not where they thought it was. That's why slow bowlers are sometimes referred to as wizards or magicians.

At the risk of boring the pants off cricketers, I need to explain a couple more things.

1. A spinning ball may bounce and turn in towards the batter (an "off break") or away from them (a "leg break"). My cunning new type of bowling was of the off break variety and proved more successful and a great deal less hard work than bowling fast.

2. A batter is "out" (ie may not bat anymore and must go back to the pavilion with their tail between their legs) if the ball hits the wicket or if they hit it and one of the other team catches it before it reaches the ground. This happened every now and again when I bamboozled an unwary batter with one of my sneaky off breaks.

To make the game more exciting, and confusing, the batter is not obliged to walk off (the position of their tail is not mandatory) until one of the pair of umpires tells them they have to. This is done by declaring that they are "out". An umpire often delays doing this until the bowler, or another member of their team, has asked them, 'How is that?' This usually comes out as a raucous 'Howzat?' The umpire responds with 'out' or 'not out'. At the very highest level, the umpire may ask video technology to do their job for them. This can take a long time, giving spectators an opportunity to nip to the bar without missing any cricket.

In 1981, I changed clubs for a third time, once more without a transfer fee. I was now playing for Middleton Stoney Cricket Club (MSCC), one of the oldest in the land and certainly one of the friendliest. The team plays in Middleton Park, a charming ground that was once part of the estate of Lord Jersey. The park's first recorded match took place in the summer of 1801, when Britain was at war with Revolutionary France, and featured Lord Jersey's Household vs the Village. Some say that events like this, symbolising the aristocracy's participation in the homespun local affairs of beef-fed yeomen, is one reason why French Revolutionary ideas did not take hold in Britain. It's hard to imagine a lace-cuffed, periwigged French Milord sitting in a gilded chair beneath a spreading oak on the boundary or taking the slightest interest in the uncouth 'Howzats?' of his snail-scoffing coachmen.

New club, new bowling style. After a few matches at Middleton Stoney I saw that my off spin was getting me nowhere. The balls I bowled were either hammered to the boundary fence (four runs to the batter without their taking a step – another quirk of the laws of cricket) or so far from the stumps that the umpire spread his arms like an albatross and called "wide" – another run to the batter without them moving their feet.

The answer to my bowling meltdown was to switch from off spin to leg spin. This is a bowler's last chance saloon. The extremely tricky technique involves twisting one's wrist like a circus contortionist and sending the ball looping in the air like a slow-flying hand-grenade. The batter either licks their lips and bashes the ball into orbit or is totally bamboozled and watches in dismay as the ball spins gently into the "stumps" (another name for the three pieces of wood, aka "wicket", which also means ... let's not go there). The great advantage for me was that few batters, especially younger ones, had seen leg spin before, and by the time they realised what it was they were out!

MSCC proved to be just my sort of club. A couple of quotes from their website should explain why.

> We have more than 30 playing members ranging in age from under twenty to over seventy who play at a wide variety of ability levels ... Selection is not based on playing merit but rather on a desire to try to match the playing strength of our opponents and give everyone a fair share of games ... Our genuine desire to compete, excel and to win is finely balanced with the heartfelt sense that we're also playing to have fun and enjoy the game in the spirit with which it's intended to be played. A "close win" and a "great match" is always the object of any fixture.

There you have it: have fun and enjoy it might well be the motto of my life. We played against some semi-serious teams, such as The Law Society and the Northamptonshire Amateurs, and also some less serious ones with eccentric names like the Invalides, Monk's Marvels and, my favourite of all, the Fallow Bucks. A match with the Fallows invariably involved a visit from their celebrity non-playing member, the actor David Tomlinson, best known for his starring roles in the movies *Mary Poppins* and *Bedknobs and Broomsticks*. Lest it be hit by a flying cricket ball, he parked his gleaming Rolls-Royce (number plate DT4) well away from the boundary, declaring that he didn't want 'one of your lusty blacksmiths denting my favourite motor.'

When David was around, the cricket took second place. Everyone he encountered, be they the lady who made sandwiches, the man who kept the score, or the club captain, was greeted as 'Darling!' Some of the older members found this a little strange, even alarming, and my strait-laced stepfather (Winchester College, Oxford, Army) was still muttering 'Darling? Darling?' as he drove away from the ground three hours later. And woe betide anyone who attempted to steal David's thunder. I tried, of course, only to be met with a sharp, 'I'll do the jokes if you don't mind Charlie!'

It was all very typical of bucolic English bonhomie: tea and sandwiches, jugs of Pimm's, barbeques after the match, yards of ale to be swallowed in one go by batters who were out to the first ball they faced (known as a "golden duck"), and cricket tours to other parts of the UK and, once, to Amsterdam. Every now and again we found the opposition had recruited a former first-class cricketer to their ranks, men like the South African test match batsman Daryll Cullinan and the seriously fast bowler John Dye.

I don't recall how I coped with the likes of Cullinan and Dye – pretty feebly, I imagine – but I do remember as if it were yesterday a match against another visiting team whose line-up included one of my all-time sporting heroes.

In the mid-1970s, English cricket was going through a rough patch. The fast bowlers of Australia and the West Indies were ripping through our batters with painful ease when the selectors, almost in despair, turned to a grey-haired man with spectacles and asked him to hold the fort, whatever the cost. And he did. His glasses remained intact, but that was about all as he survived barrage after barrage of the most hostile bowling imaginable. Photographs of his bruised body were shown in every newspaper, he became a national hero overnight, and was chosen as the 1975 BBC Sports Personality of the Year. Appropriately enough, his name matched his steadfast personality: David Steele.

I feared the worst when this man of steel came out to face my bowling. After glancing anxiously towards the pristine paintwork of the opposition's cars, I took a deep breath, walked in a few steps, swung my arm, and sent down one of my slow, lobbing leg breaks. The crowd held its breath. The BBC Sports Personality of the Year took a decisive step forward, raised his bat – and patted the ball gently back to me. He did the same to the next ball and the three after that.

Then it happened …

Deciding he had had enough of being tied down by an ageing bowler of lollipops, David lifted his bat and sent the ball soaring into the warm afternoon sunshine. If the batter strikes the ball over the boundary without it touching the ground, they are awarded six runs, the maximum possible from one blow. This is clearly what David had in mind. On the other hand, as I've explained, if someone from the bowler's team catches the ball before it touches the ground or crosses the boundary, the batter is out. David's strike launched the ball very high – high enough to send the rooks in the trees behind the pavilion cawing into the air – but not very far in terms of distance, certainly not as far as the boundary. As it came down, gathering speed as it went, one of our best catchers stationed himself beneath it.

'Mine!' he called confidently.

This was it! The finest moment of my cricketing career was upon me. In my mind I rehearsed the story for my grandchildren, how I once got out the man whom all Australia could not shift. I even planned to have the feat carved onto my tombstone. Down, down, down came the ball, into the hands of the catcher – yes, into the safe hands of the catcher, then out again. He dropped it.

'Sorry Charlie. Don't worry, I'll get him next time.'

'No problem, Ian. Good effort.'

There wasn't a next time, of course. My golden cricketing opportunity had come and gone. A few years later, I was called up to play for the prestigious Marylebone Cricket Club (MCC) and removed seven of the ten young batters of Cokethorpe School 1st XI for just eleven runs. Though that was satisfying, it did little to assuage the memory of the dismissal that never was.

The MCC, guardian of the worldwide cricketing community and keeper of the game's laws, is based at Lord's, a delightful ground (stadium) in north-west London. The MCC/Lord's set-up is a curious mix of tradition and modernity, exclusivity and inclusivity.

For two hundred and eleven years the MCC was an all-male club, admitting women only after a hard-fought battle; Lord's still hosts matches between Eton and Harrow, two of Britain's most privileged and expensive private schools, and the dress code in its pavilion is notoriously strict (or old-fashioned, depending on one's point of view): men must wear "ties and tailored coats and acceptable trousers with appropriate shoes" and women "dresses; or skirts or trousers worn with blouses, and appropriate shoes."

And yet ... Cricket is, and always has been, colour-blind; a cricket match, especially at village level, is a classless occasion; and in the many parts of the world where cricket is played seriously, from the Caribbean to Afghanistan, prowess with bat or ball is one of the few routes out of poverty for men and (in all but the most extreme religious communities) women.

I am proud to be a member of the MCC and even prouder to be part of the Lord's Taverners, a "leading youth cricket and disability sport charity" that uses cricket to "empower young people facing the challenges of inequality." The

Taverners runs a team for which, as the sun set on my cricketing career, witnessed my final appearances at the wicket. Fortunately for me, though numerous superb players turned out for the Taverners, the matches were not taken too seriously, and no one minded when an ageing and very average former member of Berkhamsted School 3rd XI turned out alongside cricketing internationals like Mike Gatting and David Gower, all-rounders like Rob Andrew, and rugby stars like Will Greenwood.

As a gesture of thanks for being allowed to play for the Taverners, I sometimes wear their colours when appearing on TV. This led to the following amusing exchange of emails.

Charlie/Is that a Yorkshire Regiment tie that you wear on *Bargain Hunt*?/Regards/ Rob Cripps

My reply:

Hello Rob/I'm afraid it's not so prestigious. It's the Lord's Taverners!!/With best wishes/Charlie

Rob's response:

I'm equally impressed. It still is a good-quality tie./Thank you for your reply./Regards/Major (Ret) Rob Cripps Ex Yorkshire Regiment

In my work as an auctioneer and valuer, nothing gives me greater pleasure than dealing with cricket-related objects. I have sold ancient paintings of cricketers looking like characters from *Pride and Prejudice*, bats signed by names that are evoked in hushed tones of reverence in the halls of cricketing celebrity, and balls kept as souvenirs of famous victories. Only once have I conducted an auction of lots comprising nothing but cricketing memorabilia. What a joy it was – and, it must be said, what a success!

The sale arose because the outspoken Robin Marlar, a fine cricketer and writer of the old school, was thinking of going to live in France and needed to offload some of his possessions. Why he thought of moving to a country where cricket is almost never played was a mystery – perhaps he saw himself as a sort of cricketing missionary, a Dr Livingstone in pads and box? That is where I came in. Robin was told he could either put his collection in the hands of a well-known London auction house or he could hire a freelance auctioneer and hold the sale in a place of his choosing.

To keep things under his personal control, he opted for the latter. The auctioneer, a chap he recognised from *Bargain Hunt* (Robin was a keen fan), suggested he work for a straight fee rather than a more complicated commission arrangement. Robin accepted. As things turned out, it proved to be the right decision – though more for one party than the other!

The venue was Sussex County Cricket Ground in Hove. Fresh from Cambridge University, Robin had played for Sussex between 1951 and 1968, captaining the side 1955–1959. He then moved into journalism, becoming cricket correspondent for *The Times* of London and writing an attractively illustrated *Story of Cricket* (1979). Whether on paper or in conversation, no one was left in any doubt as to his views about politics (Conservative, anti European Union) and social matters (men and women should not play cricket together)! He was President of the MCC, 2005–2006. After a career like this, I was unsurprised by the rich range and rarity of the objects he was selling.

My introduction to Robin had been effected by the cricketing aficionado Jon Filby. He valued the collection, produced a catalogue and, optimistically, we set up a bank of phones. Cricketing memorabilia, we were told, was going out of fashion. Robin's proved to be a startling exception. Most items went for well over their catalogue estimates, some fetching extraordinary prices. Here are some examples.

- R.D. Beeston St Ivo's account of the 1882–1883 Ashes

series in Australia sold for £3,000. The estimate had been £800–£900. (The "Ashes" is a series of matches played between England and Australia. The name originated with a mock obituary in *The Sporting Times* bemoaning England's first ever defeat by Australia in England (1882) which said English cricket had died, and "the body will be cremated and the ashes taken to Australia.")

- William Burgess's watercolour "Kent vs All England at Canterbury", dated c.1855, expected to fetch £800–£1,000, sold for £9,000.

- An oil painting of Trent Bridge, Nottinghamshire County Ground, c.1885, by H.E. Russell we reckoned would fetch £800–£1,000: I brought the gavel down at £10,000.

- H. Royston's lithograph of Robin Marlar's old school, Harrow, c.1860, was estimated to fetch £200–£250: the buyer paid £3,200.

- My favourite item was a hand-coloured lithograph of "The Eleven of England" created for "The Great Cricket Matches of the North", 1847: Ian and I thought £500–£600 was about the right price, but it went for £2,800.

- Possibly the oldest lot was an oil painting from the late 18th century depicting a cricket match between the Kent and Sussex County teams, with the names of the players added later. Robin admired the work, which had once hung behind the desk of the Sussex club secretary, and when it came up for sale in 1980 he paid £260 for it. He was clearly not the painting's only admirer. Valued in the catalogue at £2000–£3000, the bidding finally came to a halt at a startling £34,000.

I'm not sure I can explain the difference between the

suggested prices and those reached at auction. Perhaps it was a mark of the esteem in which Robin Marlar was held? Whether that was the case or not, I probably would have benefitted from the advice of Richard Madley, a *Bargain Hunt* colleague and one of our leading valuers of sporting artifacts and memorabilia. No regrets, however, as the vendor made a lot more than he had expected and afterwards made a generous donation to the Sussex Cricket Museum.

Incidently, Robin never did move to France. The thought of trying to explain a googly on a boulodrome had obviously been too dreadful to contemplate.

CHAPTER FIFTEEN

By Elephant to the Subcontinent

When a member of the public recognises me from the TV and comes up for a chat, they invariably ask one of two questions: 'Are you the man from the telly?' or 'Want to buy an elephant?'

The first is easily answered (except when they've mistaken me for my look-alike brother). I am sometimes tempted to make a facetious reply to the second question, but don't. I shake them warmly by the hand and I say how pleased I am to meet a fan of *Antiques Road Trip*. When they then say something about the famous elephant incident, I explain how it was as much a matter of luck as judgement. It began, in fact, with the spin of a coin.

The story comes from an episode of STV's *Antiques Road Trip* that I made over a decade ago. James Braxton and I were pottering around north-east Scotland in a surprisingly reliable open-top Sunbeam Alpine (c.1963). The area brought back vivid memories of family camping holidays amid the sand dunes of Findhorn, especially swimming in the freezing North Sea and watching my father try to make a cup of tea with a wheeze he had discovered for boiling water using only a couple of sheets of newspaper.

One of our stops was in the charming town of Nairn. If that means little to those whose Scottish geography is a bit hazy, we were fifty-five miles east of Inverness and sixty-six miles north of Balmoral. Yes, remote. I was struggling to compete with James, a cheerful old hand from *Flog It!* and *Bargain Hunt* who had recently set up the successful Fine Art Auction Group, and certainly knew his stuff. On arriving in Nairn, we parked outside Auldearn Antiques and took stock. As the business operated out of a converted chapel and its attendant outhouses, James and I tossed to decide who would go where. I lost and got an outhouse.

'Bad luck, Charlie,' said James kindly as he headed for the chapel. Little did he realise ...

Yorkshire folk are renowned for their pithy sayings. I have already cited one and at this point a second comes to mind: Where there's muck, there's brass. It could never have been more appropriate than in Auldearn Antiques. Entering the outhouse, I ran my eye over shelves laden with a colourful assortment of bric-a-brac and semi-precious antiques. *Hmm*, I thought, checking the prices carefully written on neat labels and stickers. *Not much chance of a bargain here. The guy who runs the place obviously knows his business.*

I was about to ask whether he'd bring down the price on a brass door knocker when my eye fell upon something odd tucked away on a table in the corner. *Wait a minute! What's that?*

It was a piece of Staffordshire pottery, the like of which I had never seen before. About nine inches tall, it represented an adult Indian elephant with a mahout perched on its neck. The mahout was a smartly dressed chap in yellow trousers with a kind of policeman's helmet on his head. I liked the look of him. I liked even more what was behind him. On top of a regular howdah towered a red brick castle, complete with battlements. In true Staffordshire style, the side walls of the castle were bizarrely decorated with a large clock face.

I scoured my brain. Yes, I knew Staffordshire earthenware – crude but fun. Collectable, too, for those who like that sort of thing, especially if it's early 19th century, which this appeared to be. The item was distinctly unusual. Bargain time.

Not wishing to be too eager, I told the owner, known locally as "Big Roger", that I had a soft spot for Staffordshire pottery. He agreed. Yes, some of it was attractive. I mentioned the elephant and howdah, adding, 'Pity it's been knocked about a bit, Roger.'

He looked at me carefully. 'Aye, but it's old, Charlie. Been around for a few years.'

'It looks like it. Picked it up as part of a house clearance, I suppose?'

'Aye. Stuffed away at the back of a cupboard.'

I held up the label. 'And you're asking twelve pounds?'

'A bargain price, Charlie.'

It certainly was. By now I had got the measure of the piece and was pretty sure at auction it would fetch more than £12. If the right buyer came along, it might get to £150 or even £250.

I looked at the elephant again. 'Tusk broken, poor thing. I'll tell you what, as it cost you nothing, I'll give you two pounds.'

'No!'

'Oh dear! Six then?'

'You'll need to go higher than that, Charlie.'

'Alright. How about eight pounds?'

After a bit more chat, the deal was struck and my £8 Staffordshire pottery elephant, complete with jolly mahout and clock-faced castle, was sent to the auction rooms at Buckie for entry in their next sale. Lot 171.

What happened next is perhaps too well known to bear repetition. If you are unsure, put "Charlie Ross elephant auction" into Google or YouTube and see for yourself. The sale gave me a wonderful excuse for a bit of amateur theatrics as the price soared way beyond everyone's expectations to a remarkable £2,700. The percentage difference between the sum paid for the object (£8.00) and its eventual auction price remains an *Antiques Road Trip* record.

'I suppose my *Road Trip* is now over,' exclaimed James even before the hammer had fallen on Lot 171. Though all hope of winning had gone, he maintained his sense of humour to the end. His last purchase had been an unremarkable glass celery vase for which he had paid £11. When the bidding opened, he called out cheerily, 'Shall we start at one thousand five hundred pounds?' Everyone laughed – and the vase went for £15.

On that rare occasion, game, set and match to Ross, C.G.

The story has two footnotes. The first involves Myrna Schkolne, the purchaser of Lot 171. The South African-born writer and antiques expert had fond childhood memories of elephants scoffing themselves on oranges in a game reserve. After moving to California, she began collecting a wide variety of elephant figures. Though she knew there were five of the same design as that lurking in Auldearn Antiques' outhouse, she had been unable to locate one until, browsing online, she came across the Cluny Auction online catalogue. It was, she said, 'love at first sight'. She had to get it, whatever the cost.

She rose at 5 am and booked a line for phone bidding. I imagine her phone bill was probably about the same as the price she paid for the elephant. No matter, for her final bid was accepted and the piece for which she had yearned so passionately arrived safe and sound a few weeks later. Mission accomplished.

Footnote two concerns Big Roger, the owner of Auldearn Antiques, who had sold me a £2,700 piece for just £8. Understandably, I felt a bit sorry for him. When in the vicinity of Nairn a few months later, I bought a bottle of the finest Scotch and presented it to him with my apologies.

'Apologies?' he said graciously. 'Och, there's no need for that.'

'Why ever not, Roger?'

'Because ever since that Staffordshire piece appeared on your programme, my shop has been rammed full of bargain hunters every day. Thanks to you and your elephant, Charlie, I've never been so busy. But I'm grateful for the Scotch, anyway. I'll have a wee dram to toast my good fortune!'

The Nairn-Buckie elephant was my first, somewhat tangential link with India. I had never visited the country and knew little of its geography, history or society. Imagine my surprise, therefore, when out of the blue I received an email inviting me to conduct an auction of Indian footballers.

Indian footballers? I didn't think there were many. Surely India, like me, was cricket mad? To be asked whether, in six weeks' time, I'd be free to sell footballers by auction in Mumbai sounded like a scam.

Accordingly, in my reply I asked somewhat facetiously whether it was the players' freeholds that were being put up for sale. The response brought me up short. The proposed auction was serious business, very serious business. The hugely successful idea of a player auction, used by India's premier cricket tournament, the IPL, was being employed by a similar organisation for football – the Indian Super League (ISL).

To be invited to conduct this auction was a considerable honour. Nevertheless, I was a little anxious. Why me rather than an Indian auctioneer? What about my trademark banter: how well does sense of humour cross national and cultural boundaries? I could just about get away with it, just about, in the US, but in India? I would need to be on my very best behaviour.

The trip taught me five important lessons about India and its people.

Lesson 1: Indians play football, serious football.

Lesson 2: Indians like to haggle. My years in the antique business had showed me how to bargain, and I thought I was quite good at it. But only when I came to arrange my contract with the ISL did I realise what an amateur I was. The average stall holder in the Hyderabad bazaar would have had me for breakfast, lunch and tea. Guided by advice from Richard Madley, the IPL auctioneer, I asked for fifty percent of my fee up front. They responded with twenty-five percent. Eventually, after I'd emailed a somewhat terse "no fee – no fly", we came to an arrangement, and I found myself comfortably seated on a British Airways flight bound for Mumbai.

Lesson 3: My preconceptions of India, fuelled largely by the films I'd seen, were correct. The extraordinarily vibrant country is both "teeming" and "steaming". The teeming bit was confirmed as my chauffeur-driven car honked and swerved its way through the jam-packed streets of Mumbai. The steaming hit me in the short walk from the car to the doors of the splendid five-star hotel where I was staying. *This place is hot*, I thought, *and in more than a meteorological sense*. Confident and chaotic, the air was filled with the frenzied self-confidence of a country on the make.

The sense of excitement was very much in evidence during the auction. The ISL had been established with eight teams, each based in a state or large city: Bangalore, Delhi, Goa, Guwahati, Kochi, Kolkata, Mumbai, and Pune. They were backed by high-profile franchises whose probity had been verified by the respected British professional services group, Ernst & Young.

A team was allowed no more than one internationally renowned superstar player, known with a strange tent-like symbolism as a "marquee". The Kerala Blasters snapped up the former England goalkeeper David James, while the former Swedish international Freddie Ljungberg went to Mumbai City.

In 2015, the distribution of India's top ten home-grown footballers among the teams was to be decided by auction. That's where I came in.

I am unusually nervous, not because the event is screened live to an estimated audience of ten million, but because I am overawed by those representing the eight franchises. Seated before me, only feet away, are some of my greatest sporting heroes. The incomparable batsman Sachin Tendulkar is with the Kochi franchise, and the outstanding all-rounder Sourav "Dada" Ganguly is part of the Kolkata franchise. On the other tables sit a breathtaking array of Bollywood goodlookers, including John Abraham, Ranbir Kapoor and Salman Khan.

The event is staged with full Bollywood razzmatazz. When all is ready, stunningly beautiful assistants bring onto the stage a football-shaped drum. Inside is a velvet sack containing the names of the ten star players. I plunge my hand into the sack and, with a suitable flourish, draw forth a token with a name on it and read it out. It's not unlike the Bucknell village Christmas tombola, just that there's a bit more riding on it.

Lesson 4: Like a newsreader or sporting commentator, have all names prepared meticulously in advance. If necessary, practise them for hours in front of the bathroom mirror.

Back in Mumbai, "Rino Anto" and "Robin Singh" present no problems. I pause a little before "Karanjit Singh" and "Jackichand Singh", covering my hesitation with a quip about how there was going to be a lot of singing in the stands. I'm relieved to find it goes down well.

Wondering if I've won my first Bollywood contract, I plunge my hand in again. Out comes "Anas Edathodika". To the audience's amusement, I manage the five-syllable surname only with a bit of prompting from one of the glamorous assistants. The audience's tolerance and sense of humour play a major part in the show's apparent success.

Once a name is announced and before I can start the bidding, the appetites of potential purchasers are whetted with a video clip of the player's finest moments. 'Look how he glides past three defenders and tips it neatly over the goalkeeper!' 'Isn't that the finest free kick you've ever seen?' And 'If all players tackled like him, every game would end nil-nil.' Etc, etc.

After the glitz, the bidding goes well, with all ten players fetching more than their reserve. I even manage (Lesson 5) to master the unfamiliar climb from single rupees to lakhs (100,000 rupees, idiosyncratically written as 1,00,000) and the dauntingly large crore (100 lakh or 10,000,000 rupees, written as 1,00,00,000). The top price is Rs 1.05 crore paid by Mumbai City FC for Sunil Chhetri.

The conclusion of each sale is an excuse for yet more showbiz hype. As soon as I bring my hammer down on a player (so to speak), a door opens at the back of the stage and the golden-booted footballer himself appears to thunderous applause, blaring music and a blitz of flashing lights. A member of the successful franchise then joins his new acquisition for an interview. Yes, they both agree, they are the most fortunate men on the planet.

And so on to the next player. Though it's only ten lots,

it's extremely hard work. When the last player has been sold, I think, *Thank God that's done!* and prepare to return to the peace and quiet of my hotel room. There might even be a bit of cricket on TV ...

But no! It's time for the press conference. I'm ushered into a large room with hundreds of flashing cameras, lights, music, and so forth. I stand behind a microphone and listen to the others discussing the respective merits of the players, how much has been paid for them, and the prospects for the upcoming season. Unable to contribute anything meaningful on such topics, I witter on as politely as I can about how exciting the auction was and how I'd love to be invited back.

I wasn't.

CHAPTER SIXTEEN

Hunting Bargains

The BBC programme *Bargain Hunt*, on air since 2000, is the only antiques programme I have taken part in that is sufficiently well known to be parodied. In 2003, CITV had a laugh with "Garbage Hunt", presented by "David Dustbin". As I didn't join until 2018 and the targeted binman was David Dickinson, who left the show in 2003, I renounce all association with garbage or refuse collectors. Quite the contrary. My time on the show has been, like almost everything else I have done since leaving school, both enjoyable and interesting – without a dustcart in sight!

For those who don't know *Bargain Hunt*, the key to its success, like that of *Antiques Roadshow*, is the variety brought by public participation (and the charm of the presenters, of course!). There is a limit to the number of times one can watch Charlie Ross trying to make a profit from buying bits and pieces, no matter how wrong he gets things. In *Bargain Hunt*, the buying at an antiques fair is done by two teams – Red and Blue – comprising two members of the public and an antiques expert advisor. Both teams are furnished with the same amount of cash. If their purchases sell at auction for more than they paid for them, they keep the difference. Though the sums involved are not bank-breaking, the challenge always makes highly entertaining viewing.

To increase its TV appeal, the programme has been tweaked over the years. Audiences have been offered primetime and daytime versions, celebrity editions (a sporting one featured Olympic gold medallists Kelly Holmes and Sally Gunnell v boxer Henry Cooper and shot-putter/strongman Geoff Capes), increases in the funds given to teams, and occasionally editions with special rules.

I have participated in two capacities. First, as an expert offering guidance to one of the teams, and latterly as one of its carousel of presenters. After my somewhat chequered career as an antiques dealer, it is hugely reassuring to work with team members who know even less about old bits and pieces than I do. As a presenter of the show, I am expected to chat for a short time about a museum, stately home or other place of historical interest in the vicinity and discuss some of the items on show there. This expanded the historical knowledge I had picked up from *Antiques Road Trip*, so that when a piece of silver is proclaimed "Georgian" I can now distinguish one chubby Hanoverian from another and slot them into the correct half century. In heaven – or the other place – I intend to have a stab at O-Level history.

Talking of the Georges reminds me of an experience I had a while back on the other side of the Atlantic. I didn't realise at the time, but *Bargain Hunt* is shown in several countries around the world, including the US. This led to an unusual Californian encounter.

After leaving the podium where I had been selling Ferraris and Rolls-Royces for David Gooding in Pebble Beach, I was approached by an elderly gentleman with a broad Southern accent and a shoelace necktie. I have forgotten the details, but the conversation went something like this:

'Say, Charlie,' he began, 'I like the way you do it.'

'Thank you very much, sir. It's pretty hard going up there with all those sharp minds –'

'No, no, Charlie,' he interrupted. 'I'm not talking about the car nuts. What gets me is how you talked that lady from Cirencester, or some place, into buying that mug with King George the Seventh on it. How the heck did you know?'

After a hard day's auctioning my brain was not exactly in overdrive, and I fumbled in the memory bag to see if there was anything there. Nothing but a few biscuit crumbs. 'Er, excuse me, sir,' I said slowly, fumbling for a clue, 'but I'm not sure ... George the Seventh ... Isn't he ... I mean, not yet –'

'Maybe it wasn't the Seventh, Charlie. What the heck, they're all the same. But that dirty old mug in a low-down antique fair – you wouldn't have gotten me to buy it, no sir!'

The fog began to clear. Yes, I did vaguely recall persuading a woman on *Bargain Hunt* that a George V coronation mug in good condition was worth something.

'The coronation of George V took place in June 1911,' I explained, 'so the mug was more than a century old.'

'Yeah, looked it. Like I said, you sure sold it strong.'

I explained that I hadn't sold it, just advised the contestant that it might be a wise purchase. But how come he had seen an episode of *Bargain Hunt*? Presumably, it was on holiday in the UK?

'Vacation over there? No, never been out of the US. Can't say I want to, either. But I like your TV.'

'Thank you.'

'Good to meet you, Charlie. And well done with that mug.' With that, he turned and sauntered off to chat to someone else.

Pausing to reflect on the incident, I registered two

takeaways: one, *Bargain Hunt* was showing in the US; two, I knew more history than I thought I did, and began to daydream. O-Level history? Huh! Child's play. What I should do is a degree. Get some letters after my name: Charles Ross BA or MA or, why not, PhD? Miles better than RICS.

Then I woke up.

On another overseas *Bargain Hunt* occasion a man in Canton, China, grasped me warmly by the hand and repeated, 'Oh *Bargain Hunt*! Oh *Bargain Hunt*!' over and over again. I smiled politely and said what a pleasure it was to meet him. His accent was so thick that only afterwards did it dawn on me what he had been saying.

My most memorable experience as a presenter of *Bargain Hunt* occurred in 2018. It was a celebrity edition for BBC's Music Day, featuring the popstar, writer, DJ and actor Jarvis Cocker versus Bez, the instrumentalist, singer, songwriter and member of the band Happy Mondays. Jarvis's team partner was Candida Doyle from the band Pulp, Bez's was Rowetta Idah from Happy Mondays.

Advising Jarvis was not easy. I suggested that the less than accomplished painting he described as 'a semi-nudist camp somewhere' might not fetch a lot at auction. He turned down my advice – and it didn't. At the end of the auction he and Rowetta were down £95. No hope of them winning, surely? All Bez and Candida had to do was play it straight …

At the end of shooting they appeared to have done so and were home and dry with a profit of £8. Then the team viewing the rushes of the day's filming noticed something odd. Rowetta was seen bidding for her team partner's lots, thereby pushing up the price. The rules of the competition forbade bidding by friends or family members, and, having broken the rules, Bez was disqualified and obliged to pay back the £8.

Jarvis and his tasteless depiction of a semi-nudist camp

were declared the winners. Actually, the real winner was *Bargain Hunt* after the massive publicity the episode received!

Business and pleasure, they say, don't mix. Well, as you may have gathered, for me they mix all the time. They are, in fact, inseparable. I honestly can't see the point of spending one's life doing something one doesn't enjoy. For instance, I enjoy singing and I enjoy auctioneering. The two don't have a lot in common, of course, except once, in December 2017, when they came together in surprisingly tuneful harmony.

It would be nice to think that we came up with the idea ourselves, but we didn't. That honour must go to Graham Corbyn of Saga Entertainment. What, he wondered, might four *Bargain Hunt* experts – James Braxton, Charles Hanson, Philip Serrell and myself – do for Children in Need? An edition of the show dressed in yellow bear suits? Not terribly exciting. Wearing our underpants over our trousers? No! 1950s schoolboy humour had no appeal in the 21st century and might well put people off giving to the cause. So, what *could* this quartet of experts in the ancient do that would appeal to a 21st-century audience? There must be something …

Then came Graham's brainwave. Could we sing? he asked. At this prompt, I began to hum. Charles Hanson, sitting next to me, smiled and took up the tune, followed by James Braxton and Philip Serrell. That was it! We all liked music and could sing a bit. Perhaps, Graham asked, we could record and release a Christmas single? Someone might buy it, and the money would go to charity.

We went through the seasonal repertoire. "White Christmas"? Too difficult and perhaps a bit corny. A well-known carol? Might not appeal to everyone. In the end we chose a rock version of "Sleigh Ride" by Leroy Anderson and Mitchell Parish. Unwilling to launch us on the public unaccompanied, Graham teamed us up with his Christmas ensemble, many of whom were – unlike us – extremely accomplished singers. A day was booked at the Metropolis Studios, Chiswick, London, where four middle-aged men in headphones had the time of their lives pretending to be rock stars. When it was all over, they went down to the pub to ease their strained vocal cords.

'Well, it was fun while it lasted,' I ventured over a pint of London Pride. The others agreed.

To our amazement, that was only the beginning. Our digital "Sleigh Ride" reached a hat trick of number 1 slots: momentarily top of the Amazon Rock Charts, the Amazon Rock Best Sellers, and the Amazon Hot New Releases Chart. I still smile at the thought of having been a "hot new release" at the age of sixty-seven!

I also appeared on the fun TV show *Put Your Money Where Your Mouth Is* (2008–2017), produced by Reef Television for the BBC. It had a more generous budget than most antiques gameshows, even sending me across the Channel for one episode. Having spent many delightful holidays in France, I have developed a sincere affection for that country, its people, and its glorious gastronomy. Only once in my experience did French life bear any resemblance to that depicted in the TV series *'Allo! 'Allo!* or by Peter Sellars as Inspector Clouseau in the brilliant *Pink Panther* films. The occasion occurred when *Put Your Money Where Your Mouth Is* took me to Paris with Eric Knowles, a long-standing expert from the *Antiques Road Show*.

We went to an antiques fair somewhere in the suburbs – I forget the precise location – where I was invited to wander around to see if I could spot a bargain or two. One stall in particular took my interest. Small and shabby, it comprised a bare wooden table before a glass-fronted cabinet containing assorted pieces of interesting-looking silverware. I approached and prepared to introduce myself.

The two middle-aged men looking after the stall, both wearing archetypal blue berets, were seated at a table smoking cigars. Each had a glass of red wine in one hand which they topped up from time to time from a bottle on the table. There were two more bottles beneath beside their feet, both unopened. Rather than doing their best to attract customers, the pair were engrossed in a game of backgammon. Their only movement, apart from rolling the dice and shifting the counters, was the occasional Gallic shrug; their only conversation a mumbled 'Zut alors!' or 'Merde!' To the casual passer-by, they were as disconnected from the world around them as the silver figurine of a shepherdess in the cabinet behind them. Less animated, too.

I peered into the mists of time to see if there was anything remaining from my O-Level French (grade 3).

'Bonjour messieurs!'

No response.

'Je suis Charlie Ross de la programme Placer Votre Argent Ou Est Votre Bouche. Je suis looking pour objects acheter.'

The man on my left gave me a quizzical look, put down his glass, waved his hand in a gesture that could have meant anything from Shove off, idiot! to Take a look if you must. Picking up his glass, he refocussed on the backgammon.

I opted for the latter interpretation of the hand signal and moved towards the cabinet.

'Votre argent est jolie, messieurs.'

Again, no response.

I was about to open the cabinet when a second customer appeared. I stood back and watched as he swung back the glass doors and looked inside. He clearly knew his stuff. After a quick scan of the contents, he reached out, picked up a small, fluted cream jug, and checked the markings on the bottom.

To my astonishment, he then turned to me and asked, 'Combien pour cette pièce, monsieur?'

On occasions like this one does not always do what one ought to do. Instead of telling him that I was nothing to do with the stall but simply a guy from a British TV programme, I shrugged and raised my hands, palms upwards, in what I hoped signalled *Not a clue, you tell me.*

He did. 'Je vous offre cinquante, monsieur.'

Cinquante? What the hell was that? Un, deux, trois … Ah yes, fifty. Fifty euros at 8.5 to the pound is roughly 43 pounds. Too cheap!

'Mais non, monsieur. Soixante.'

'Soixante?'

'Oui monsieur, soixante. Un bargain!'

He gave me a strange look before counting out sixty euros from his jacket pocket and thrusting them into my hand. 'Une bargain,' he smiled. With that, he picked up the jug and walked off.

To this day I will never know whether it was une bargain or not. When I placed the sixty euros on the table beside the backgammon board and left with a cheery 'au revoir', neither of the players showed any interest whatsoever.

Zut alors indeed!

CHAPTER SEVENTEEN
An Alien of Extraordinary Ability

At the time, it wasn't altogether obvious that the interest in cars bequeathed to me by my father would prove more useful to me than his broken hearing aid and worn Spanish trainers. But that's how it turned out. My ability to distinguish between a Fiat and a Ferrari, to explain that Karl Benz's business partner, Emil Jellinek, had a daughter named Mercedes, and to state that, before the introduction of speed limits, Uncle Mac's Jag Mk II 3.4 had been clocked at 140 mph on the M1 motorway, enabled me to sound moderately knowledgeable when chatting with David Gooding about his new vintage car business in Pebble Beach, California.

David ran the International Motor Car Department of Christie's before working with Peter Bainbridge, principal auctioneer at RM Auctions (now RM Sotheby's, the world's largest vintage and classic car auction business). In 2004, with Christie's no longer under contract at Pebble Beach, the site was offered to David. It was an exceptional opportunity. David was experienced in business, knew the trade inside out, and had lots of useful contacts – so he went for it. It didn't take him long to sort out the logistics and line up some fine classic and vintage cars for auction. The missing piece of the Pebble Beach jigsaw was the auctioneer.

That, as I explained at the beginning of this strange, eventful history, was how my Great American Adventure began.

I am ashamed to confess that I knew next to nothing about the United States before I went there. Rather, I knew next to nothing of the sprawling, complex cassoulet of contradictions that is the true US. Instead, like many citizens of the 20th-century world, I had a vivid image of what the country was like. My picture, drawn largely from my early childhood experiences, was reinforced by movies, with additional material from songs, newsreels and the country's endless stream of ingenious, over-sized products. By the age of twelve it was fixed in my mind.

My US was a land of color [sic] beside black-and-white Britain. Where we were old, war-torn and tired, America was new and bursting with energy. We looked back, unsure of our place among nations; Americans looked forward, certain that they could forge a brave new world in their image. Yet it wasn't all positive–negative. We allowed ourselves a small pat on the back by knowing smugly that they were brash and amusingly naïve, while we were cultured and immensely sophisticated. That was our thin, morale-boosting lifeline.

This early one-dimensional image of the US was fostered by my mother, who lauded America and its people to the skies. Her outlook stemmed from her wartime experience when she was billeted in a requisitioned country house with USAF pilots. She didn't speak much about her experiences – she was, after all, a married woman – but an annual Christmas card from a certain Stafford Parker, postmarked Vermont, may have had something to do with her unshakeable affection for the land of the free.

I met my first Americans around the age of four. We were living in a flat in Brayfield House (another of my mother's posh addresses – no pavements, no numbers) in the village of Cold Brayfield. The place was abuzz with larger-than-life eccentrics. The lodge at the entrance to the drive was let to Col Paul Rodzianko, a White Russian émigré who, having served with the British Military Mission to Russia, conducted riding lessons from his armchair by barking commands to terrified pupils through a megaphone. The house itself was owned by Michael Farrer, supposedly a blood relative of King Henry VIII. His reputation as a socialite tearaway lends some credence to this alleged ancestry. Somewhere upstairs lived the Honourable Joan Farrer (née Mitford). I remember almost nothing about her other than she was unusual and, we were warned, to be avoided. Not so the lively USAF pilot and his young family who leased a large downstairs flat on the ground floor.

What a cave of undreamed-of delights it was! The apartment and its smiling inhabitants were all large, warm, loud, and smelt of peanut butter. They were generous, too. At Christmas they gave me a pop gun rifle (one barrel) when Father Christmas had left me only a Dinky Toy car. The thrill was slightly lessened when Stewart unwrapped his pop gun – double-barrelled. In the spring, I forgot the slight when Stewart walked across the fields to Newton Blossomville Primary School, leaving me – not yet of school age – free to go into the conservatory and play Micky Mouse, Donald Duck and Pluto cartoon games with our American neighbours' three- and four-year-old daughters. I can't remember whether I was a mouse, a dog or a duck, but I do remember how enthralled I was by their authentic accents.

These were the memories, polished by John Wayne, Technicolor and Cecil B. DeMille, that floated in my mind as

I applied for a visa to enter the US half a century later. Assassinations, wars and riots had tarnished the image but failed to obliterate it. I remained convinced of the essential polite wholesomeness of the US, and I still am.

In my early days of transatlantic travel, the intimidating immigration and customs officers at Los Angeles International Airport did their best to disillusion me. After one visit, I wondered whether I was the only visitor to the US who believed the border control service had scoured the country for suitably sour-faced recruits? I had fun imagining their job adverts, which ran something like this ...

- Do you believe in the Fall of Man?

- However tempted, are you able to resist smiling for at least six hours?

- Can you *guarantee* to have forgotten the manners your parents taught you?

If you can give an unqualified YES to these questions, the US Immigration Service needs YOU. Apply now ...

I had this in mind when I had said to the man frowning at my passport that the purpose of my visit was a holiday. The frown changed to a scowl.

'Holiday? You here on vacation?'

'Er, vacation, yes, that's it. I'm here for a vacation.'

'Long way to come for a week's vacation.'

'Yes, you're right. I love America and wish I could stay longer, but I have to work – back in England.'

With a disbelieving 'Huh!' he stamped my passport and waved me in.

To be fair, I should point out that my recent experiences with the US immigration service are completely different. Clearly a PhD in Customer Service has now been made a prerequisite for the job, for they almost board your aircraft as soon as it has landed and welcome you, coffee in hand, with cheery smiles as broad as the Grand Canyon.

The "here on vacation" line was never more than a temporary expedient. Its pink-faced inadequacy was exposed when David Gooding recommended me to Ocean Tomo, a Chicago law firm specialising in patents, who needed an auctioneer to conduct an intellectual property (IP) sale. Never having been in possession of much intellectual property myself and never having auctioned an idea before, I was interested in the concept and decided to give it a go. The firm's auction arm was run by the friendly and scarily bright Andrew Ramer, who made me very welcome and explained how an IP auction worked.

I handled several of Andrew's auctions, broadening my experience and learning about an entirely different side of the profession. Most lots generated no interest whatsoever, leaving a normally garrulous auctioneer a bit lost for words. I did my best, but there's a limit to the amount of excitement that can be generated from the concept of a nine-millimetre, spring-loaded, fire extinguisher release valve in anodised aluminium. Then, every twenty or thirty lots or so, the bidding would go crazy and a patent valued at $20,000–$30,000 would rocket up to an astonishing $2 million. If I mention that Microsoft and Google were among the bidders, you can probably understand why.

Though auctions like that can be disconcerting, my experience on touching down at San Francisco for the first time was much hairier. Frisco immigration officers, I discovered, were a few degrees sharper than their colleagues down in Los Angeles. When I was asked why I was seeking entry into the US, I gave my usual 'here on vacation' reply and prepared to walk on.

The next line could have come straight from one of those 1950s movies I had been brought up on.

'Not so fast, mister!'

Oops! Had I finally been found out?

'What's your job ... sir?'

'Job?'

'Yeah. What work do you do? You do work, don't you ... sir?'

I was beginning to feel a bit flustered. What if they wouldn't let me in? No auction = no pay. The electricity bill, the insurance, school fees ... Without thinking, I told the truth.

'Yes, I work. I'm an auctioneer.'

'Hmm ... Not auctioneering while you're over here ... sir?'

I was now bright red. 'Over here? No sir. Only in Woburn, near the Abbey ... the Duke of Bedford ...'

He put me out of my misery, muttering, 'Sure thing,' and stamping my passport. 'Have a good day ... sir.'

I thanked him, grabbed my bag from the luggage carousel, hurried out onto the sidewalk, and looked around. Directly opposite the airport entrance was a huge billboard advertising the upcoming auction, complete with a large picture of me with my name underneath.

It was time to get a visa.

David Gooding, uncomfortable at the thought of a tourist conducting his auctions, agreed and, with considerable help from immigration lawyer Richard J Tasoff, helped me start the painstakingly thorough process of obtaining a US work visa. I was flatteringly advised that the one to go for was an 0-1, meaning I was "an alien of extraordinary ability". I checked the rubric. An 0-1 was indeed,

> ... a nonimmigrant visa ... for the individual who possesses extraordinary ability in the sciences, arts, education, business, or athletics, or

who has a demonstrated record of extraordinary achievement in the motion picture or television industry and has been recognized nationally or internationally for those achievements.

Gulp.

Did I fit into any of these exalted categories? Extraordinary ability was a bit of a hurdle before I started.

Sciences – three Fs at A-Level ruled that one out.

Arts – I asked the immigration lawyer advising me whether singing the Pirate King on stage in Oxford would count.

'Professional opera singer?'

'Not quite. Amateur operetta.'

'Sorry Charlie. Covent Garden or nothing.'

Education – forget it.

Business – ditto. Downer Ross was not exactly blue chip.

That left only athletics.

'I don't suppose "occasionally effective bowler of leg breaks" would mean much to the chaps at immigration?'

'No Charlie, it wouldn't. Not to me, either.'

'Oh dear! Then we'd better try and make something of my extraordinary achievements on TV and conducting a wide variety of entertaining auctions all over the world?'

We used it, and it worked. The final dossier, over a hundred pages long, was a glowing account of my auctioneering and television career, with the ropey bits left out and the good bits polished until they shone like the torch on the Statue of Liberty. It was accompanied by snippets from programmes and embarrassingly glowing references from influential people who said I had made them laugh or inadvertently part with their money. With an 0-1 safely in my passport, David Gooding could finally breathe easy. Andrew Ramer, however, could not.

In some states, having an 0-1 visa is not enough to work as an auctioneer. In Illinois, for instance, where I had first auctioned patents, would-be gavel-bashers must first pass an examination in state auctioneering law. An examination! The very word brought me out in a cold sweat. Nevertheless, it had to be done. I sent for the vast file of case law that had to be mastered for the exam, then settled down to study it.

Two things surprised me. First, my grey cells were not quite as addled as I feared they would be. Years of auctioneering had kept them, if not fighting fit then at least able to break into a jog without collapsing, and I was able to recall facts and figures without much difficulty. Second, after I had got over the dismay of doing something that forty years previously I had sworn I would never do again, I rather enjoyed it. For the first time in my life, I was studying something that I could relate to and which I found interesting and informative. That's probably why I found it relatively easy to remember.

Moreover, the pressure was taken off by an extraordinary clause in small print at the foot of the application form: "This examination must be taken up to six months before the applicant takes the auction or up to seven days after the auction has taken place." I read it several times to make sure it meant what I thought it meant. Yes, the exam required to conduct an auction could be taken a week after the auction had finished. As it was highly unlikely that I would auction in Illinois ever again, it didn't matter whether I passed or failed. As it turned out, for almost the first time in my life, I passed.

No letters after my name yet, but I was now a proudly qualified Illinois auctioneer with an 0-1 visa to boot.

The battering my impression of the US had at the hands of its immigration service was soon repaired. On my first visit to Pebble Beach, a large and elegant car collected me at the airport and swished me to a luxurious five-star hotel. The drinks cabinet was larger than the bar at The Old Red Lion, Great Brickhill, and the bath was big enough to swim in. Never having previously experienced anything above three stars (the BBC stretch to a Premier Inn, if you're lucky), I was overwhelmed. The next morning, after a night in a bed big enough for an entire family and a breakfast that would have defeated a hippopotamus, the same car and its impeccably mannered driver ferried me to Pebble Beach.

In my childhood, family holidays were taken at Climping, midway between Bognor Regis and Littlehampton on the south coast. The beach at Climping, where we spent many happy if rather chilly days, is described as "made up of shingle and pebbles held in place by a series of wooden groynes", and I suppose at the back of my mind I had an idea that this is what Pebble Beach, California, would be like. In fact, Climping is to Pebble Beach what our family's second-hand Ford Consul was to a brand-new Cadillac. Pebble Beach is an exclusive and extremely opulent community on California's spectacular Monterey Peninsula. It comprises a small number of dwellings, stunning golf courses, a Country Club, fine restaurants, and is accessed along the world-famous 17-Mile Drive which non-residents pay to use. Lurking in the trees are some of the most sought-after parcels of real estate in the world. I had arrived in the America of my childhood fantasies.

The Gooding auctions operate out of an enormous marquee. There are in fact four marquees, three in which the cars are held for viewing on the two days prior to the auction, and a fourth, capable of holding a crowd of 1,500 for the two-day auction itself. When I say marquee, please don't imagine anything even vaguely resembling a tent, not even the type that are erected for the smartest UK weddings. The Gooding saleroom marquee is more like a cross between Victoria

Railway Station and the Alhambra Palace magically transported to a site beside the rolling Pacific Ocean. Yes, in America everything – cars, houses, refrigerators, meals and marquees – is enormous.

David introduced me to his staff (unfailingly polite and cheerful) and to his charming wife, Dawn. This cleared up what might have been an embarrassing misunderstanding. Until this moment I had assumed David was gay from his references to his wife Don. Only when I met her in person did it dawn (sorry!) on me than an American "Don" was a British "Dawn". I now thought of composer John Tavener's "Hymn of Dawn", which I had sung in our choir, in an entirely new light.

Introductions over, we set to work. David was meticulous in his attention to the cars – hardly surprising given the prices he was hoping to sell them for – and we didn't finish until around 1 am the next morning. David insisted I know the cars inside out, not just the mechanical details but their history: third in the 1966 Le Mans, rebuilt after it crashed in the 1954 Mille Miglia, and so forth. I was OK with the Ferraris, Jaguars, Alfa Romeos and other European models, but some of the American ones required a lot of hasty homework. I knew about the Ford Mustang, had heard of the Firebird Trans AM and Corvette Stingray, but the Shelby Cobra 427? A lot of swotting was required.

David also filled me in on the likely bidders, what they looked like and where they would be sitting. He showed me photographs and gave pithy character sketches. This guy has a sense of humour, for example, while this one does not (essential info for my style of auctioneering); this man will pretend to be asleep before suddenly joining in the bidding; this one has a habit of starting strong and pulling out ... and so on. It was all utterly fascinating, especially when I knew that in most cases the bidding would start at a price way beyond the upper limit at a Downer Ross sale.

On the day of the auction, a crowd of over one thousand purchasers, vendors and spectators gradually drifted in. Drinks were bought at the bar, cars inspected and old acquaintances renewed. Appearance mattered, not just because it increased the chances of a good sale but because on the Sunday after the auction, Pebble Beach would hold its spectacular Concours d'Elegance where cars from all over the world were on display, competing for prizes in a variety of categories: the coolest looking, the most polished, the unrestored vehicle in the best condition, etc.

The auction itself got under way around 6 pm. I auctioned fourteen lots of automobilia before the first car was driven onto the block beside my podium. With the occasional exception, David's cars must be in perfect working order, and he introduces each one with a brief description, embellishing the most prestigious with a bespoke video. It's then up to me to sell them.

First up was a brand-new Rolls-Royce Limited Edition Centenary Phantom, one of thirty-five built to celebrate the centenary of probably the most famous marques in the history of motoring. In the back seat, smiling broadly, was none other than Sir Stirling Moss. After this most iconic of names in motor sport had delivered a few well-chosen words, I went to work.

I sold the Rolls (excluding passenger) for $350,000, instantly obliterating my Woburn record of £66,000 for a Georgian bookcase cupboard. At Lot 35 I made my first mistake. The car was a magnificent 1921 Farman A6B Super Sport Torpedo. His Highness the Maharaja of Idar had used this vast, silver-red bullet-shaped monster for tiger hunting. (As a confirmed conservationist, I hope he was a hopeless shot.)

The bidding rose to $430,000 then stalled.

'For the first time at four hundred and thirty thousand dollars,' I called. No further bids.

'For the second time at four hundred and thirty thousand dollars.' No response.

'And for the third and last time, at four hundred and thirty thousand pounds ... ' Ah, a response! But not the sort I was expecting.

The bidder was on his feet. 'Excuse me sir, but you have just doubled my bid!'

Oops! Without realising it, I had inadvertently slipped back to Woburn and called the final bid in pounds sterling. With £1.00 being roughly the equivalent of $2.00 at the time, the bidder was right, and I was fortunate that he had a sense of humour (or, more accurately, humor). I corrected my mistake before bringing the hammer down and moving on to Lot 36.

I have talked about the highlight of my first Gooding auction in Chapter One. It only remains for me to say that, having flown home on cloud nine, I arrived jet-lagged at Downer Ross the following morning and was so useless that at midday Evan advised me to go home.

'I don't know what they did to you over there, Charlie,' he said with a wry smile, 'but if you don't mind my saying, in the state you're in now, you're no bloody use here.'

He was right. Auctioning Royal Doulton figures for forty quid each would never be quite the same again.

CHAPTER EIGHTEEN

Putters and Punters

After the successful sale of the Duesenberg Mormon Meteor and despite my attempt to sell the Maharaja's tiger-hunting wagon for twice its worth, I was retained by David Gooding and at the time of writing have conducted well over 50 auctions for him. Though the majority are in Pebble Beach, I have also enjoyed Gooding auctions in Scottsdale (Arizona), Lynchburg (Virginia), Amelia Island (Florida), and my own capital city, London. For the better part, the sales have gone very well indeed – whatever financial storms are sweeping the world, the market for fine old motors holds up remarkably well. In 2018, for example, when another 1935 Duesenberg came under the hammer, we managed to urge the bidding up to $22 million, a world record for an American car at auction.

At this point I must mention the invaluable role in all this played by my wife Sally. Whenever I conduct an auction in which there is telephone bidding (very common nowadays, especially in a country the size of the US), I ask that Sally handles one of the telephone lines. No one does it better. In contrast to the flamboyant stuff going on beside her on the podium, she is the epitome of calm efficiency, explaining clearly and concisely to the telephone bidder precisely what is happening. She was on the phone when we sold the $22-million Duesenberg, for example, handling bids of millions of dollars with the same equanimity as the weekly grocery bill. Her almost regal serenity so impresses the Gooding team that they know her as "Lady Ross".

With all this to-ing and fro-ing across the Atlantic, as well as the TV work, it was getting increasingly difficult to manage the Woburn saleroom. Eventually, in 2008 I decided it was time to let it go. A purchaser was found, I said goodbye to the staff who had been such fun to work with and drove away. Relieved, yes, but at the same time sad to leave the place where my new life in the media had started.

At an age when many people are thinking of retirement, I found myself beginning Life Part II. The prospect of stopping work held no delights for me. This was partly due to the work ethic instilled in me by my mother (who went rapidly downhill the moment she stopped working) and partly because, owing to circumstances beyond my control, I couldn't afford to retire. Appearing on TV may appear glamorous, but it is certainly not a ticket to millions! Nor is working in the US. As a British citizen employed in the US, one is obliged to pay American tax, which the Inland Revenue then takes into consideration when deciding how much tax one pays on this side of the Atlantic.

The people who buy cars for millions of dollars at a Gooding car auction fascinate me. Who are they? Well, they are mostly men and largely in their sixties or older. They are passionate about cars and, which makes my job so much easier, invariably polite and friendly. The quality I admire most about them is their self-discipline – I suppose that's why they're multi-millionaires. I am often surprised, for instance, when someone has bid $5 million for a car, they won't go to $5.2 million to secure it. The answer is definitely not shortage of funds. It must be that they have decided on a ceiling in advance and nothing will persuade them to go any higher. I wish I could be so controlled at the roulette table!

So how rich are these genial, iron-willed car fanatics? I once asked Garth Hammers, one of the Gooding specialists, about the wealth of one of our prominent purchasers who was, I was told, "into education". This was the reply.

'Well, Charlie, he owns two universities. At the first one the students pay fees of $11,000 per term. He also provides them with accommodation at $7,000 per term. That's $54,000 per student per annum. At the last count, the university had six thousand students.

'His second university has five thousand students, each paying fees of $9,000 per term and another $6,000 or so for accommodation.'

I once tried to work out what all this came to. But when I put the figures into my calculator and pressed the = button, the screen simply said "error"! After one auction, at which this punter (let's call him "Uniman") had used his credit card to buy a few cars totalling several million dollars, I congratulated him on his purchase and we fell into a lengthy chat about our mutual love of cars. In the course of our conversation, I learned that he liked to travel. Did he ever come to London? He did, sure. Where did he stay? The Savoy? The Dorchester?

'Actually,' he replied. 'We've got a little place of our own.'

'Somewhere central?'

'You know, Charlie, I always forget the name of the place.' He turned to his wife. 'Honey, where's our place in London?'

'Eaton Square.'

It wasn't a flat, either, but a three- or four-bedroom house.

The last such Eaton Square property to sell freehold (2022) went for £26 million. Uniman owned his house freehold and had a Rolls-Royce and chauffeur permanently on hand to take him and his wife around the city when he was in residence.

I have learned over time that punters like Uniman and the equally genial fellow who owned "a bit of real estate in Silicon Valley" that reputedly brought him in $30 million a month, are impossible to spot. Their unanticipated disregard for the conventional trappings of wealth has more in common with ancient British aristocrats than princes from the Gulf or Russian oligarchs. It is not uncommon to find one of these modern-day Rockefellers wandering, apparently aimlessly, around the auction room wearing shorts and trainers and munching abstractedly from a packet of Cheetos, before suddenly stopping, passing the Cheetos from the right hand to the left and putting in a bid for, say, $5 million. A man who buys a 1959 Ferrari 250 GT LWB California Spyder Competizione does not care for or need bling.

One final word about these Gooding punters. As I mentioned with regard to the man who was amused rather than annoyed when I inadvertently swapped his bid from dollars to pounds, nearly all of them have a keen sense of humour. Here is the best example to date. In my younger days, so as not to lose momentum, I used to pride myself on conducting a five- or six-hour auction non-stop. After one such marathon, a man came up to me and wondered whether he might ask me a question.

'Of course, sir. Anything you want.'

'Well, I know this is a bit personal, Charlie, but do you have a catheter up there?'

Up there? It was one of the few occasions in my life when I was completely lost for words.

For those who know the place, Pebble Beach is

synonymous with Pebble Beach Golf Links, generally rated America's top public course. I haven't played there (a round would have cost more than my generous auction commission) but I have walked on it. So have others with no golfing pretensions whatsoever: the 18th fairway is used as a display park for the post-auction Concours. But what about the tyre marks (or perhaps, as we're in the US, 'tire' marks) ask horrified British golfers? Relax. It never rains in Monterey.

I have played at Monterey's equally tricky Spanish Bay course with its spectacular sea views. My partner for the day was Andrew Ramer of Ocean Tomo (see Chapter Seventeen) who proved as precise and accurate at golf as he was at business. He won easily. Another disconcerting aspect of my Spanish Bay experience was that I was obliged to play with a caddy. This was both expensive and embarrassing. As I reached for my 3 wood for a shot off the fairway, this flattering flunkey would say such things as, 'For a young golfer like you, Charlie, I reckon it's an 8 iron from here.' I managed to prove him wrong almost every time.

I first played golf at school. The most important reason for choosing the sport was that matches, including travel, took the better part of a day and therefore meant missing lessons. This welcome perquisite fired an enthusiasm that has endured to the present day. It has important spin-offs, too. When it comes to buying a new car (always second-hand, actually – better value), to my mind the most important feature is not comfort or looks or economy, but space at the back. Will it hold a couple of sets of golf clubs?

My enthusiasm for the game was boosted when I learned, while still aspiring to join Uncle Mac in Cavendish Square, that his practice partner Ian Caldwell was the English Amateur Champion. Dentistry and golf – what an excellent life! As you know, the dentist side of things didn't last long.

The golf survived and flourished, however, further inspired by the passionate devotion to the game of my Scottish stepfather, Alexander Henderson, with whom I played many, many enjoyable rounds.

Every now and again, golf and auctioneering have coincided. This happened at Sunningdale Golf Club, one of the most prestigious in the land whose membership includes such well-known figures as the actor Hugh Grant, the footballer and TV presenter Gary Lineker and the opera singer Bryn Terfel. The club also has a reputation for being notoriously stuffy. The application for membership from Kevin Keegan, the former England football captain and manager, was rejected because members feared the clubhouse would be overrun by "people wearing white socks and shiny tracksuit bottoms."

CLIC Sargent, the historic name of Young Lives vs Cancer, a charity that raises funds for research into childhood cancer, held regular fundraising golf days at Sunningdale, and each year I was invited to run their fundraising auction. One of these gatherings is indelibly engraved on my memory. It kicked off with a match of team golf that featured stars of the game like Justin Rose and legends from other sports, such as the Irish rugby captain, Keith Wood. This was followed by a loud and boozy lunch hosted by the ebullient Eddie Jordan. Then came the auction.

The lots – including a week in a villa in Barbados – were spectacular and fetched equally spectacular prices. Only one struck me as a bit thin. After the official list had been closed, an Irishman approached me and asked for four tickets for the Gaelic Football Final to be included. I hesitated, tactfully saying that we already had sufficient lots and suggesting that perhaps a game of Gaelic Football was not to everyone's taste. I wasn't sure there would be much interest.

'Interest, Charlie?' he snorted. 'You don't know what

you're talking about. Where I come from, those tickets are rarer than hen's teeth.'

Where he came from, maybe, but this was Sunningdale not Limerick. Nevertheless, I agreed to include the tickets as an extra lot. When the time came, I opened the bidding at an optimistic £500. To my astonishment, a forest of hands shot up. I should have realised ... Eddie Jordan, Keith Wood ... the Irish were here in force, and this match was their Christmas and Birthday rolled into one. They would give anything – well, almost anything – to be there.

The brisk bidding eventually stopped at £3,000. 'For the first time,' I called – only to be interrupted by a voice from the back of the room.

'I'll make it four thousand if you drop your trousers!'

It was Aidan Heavey, former Aer Lingus financial controller and founder of Tullow Oil. Irish, of course. I was tempted, but only for a split second. A hideous image flashed before my eyes. It was the front page of the next day's *The Sun* newspaper with the glaring headline, "BBC presenter lowers standards for cash." It was followed half a second later by a second image, this on BBC-headed notepaper: "Dear Mr Ross, It has been brought to our attention that ..." However worthy the cause, I couldn't do it. It might cost me my job.

Thinking fast, I came up with an idea that would avoid outright refusal while at the same time save me from public exposure. I needed an impossible figure.

'What can I say?' I wavered. 'I'm sorry but I don't drop my trousers in public – even for a charity as worthy as this one – for less than £10,000.'

That'll do it, I thought as I prepared to press on with the auction. 'For the second time –'

A shout of 'ten thousand pounds!' cut me short. I looked up to see Dennis O'Brien, an Irishman famous for his wealth and his generosity, grinning from ear to ear.

'Come on, Charlie, take 'em down if you want your ten grand!' The rest of the room was roaring with laughter.

Hoist by my own petard, there was no escape. As I undid my belt, I desperately tried to remember what underpants I had put on that morning. Surely not that old pair of ill-fitting, once-white Y-fronts that I should have binned years ago? Trying to look as dignified as possible, I slowly lowered my trousers …

In the end, it all worked out fine. My pants were new, clean and snug, and the crowd applauded. Dennis O'Brien handed over a cheque for £10,000 saying it was the best ten grand he had ever spent. No one told *The Sun* and my job with the BBC was safe. Even more remarkably, I am still allowed to enter Sunningdale Golf Club.

Perhaps it's not so stuffy after all?

The Sunningdale pantomime was just one of over a thousand charity auctions I have conducted over the years. They range from local village hall events raising a few hundred pounds to glamorous international shows that bring in hundreds of thousands of pounds. To start with, I didn't charge for this work. Eventually, with the exception of a handful of very small fundraisers near where I live, this changed. Why? (a) I was doing so many charity auctions for nothing that I was running out of time to do my other work; (b) human nature being what it is, I find that a charity auction is taken more seriously (better organisation, prizes, etc) when the organisers know they have to fork out a little to bring in a lot – a sort of investment, and (c) the same principle probably applies to me. No matter how generous and kind-hearted I am, no matter how much I care for the charity concerned, there is a side of me that says, *Crikey! These people are paying me a bit of the takings: I'd better make it worthwhile for both of us!* And it works. Looking back, I see that in general the funds raised from professional auctions outstrip the amateur ones.

My first charity auction was a modest local affair. I can remember almost nothing about it but remain eternally grateful for whoever invited me. There, on a rainy evening in that dimly lit, gravy-smelling hotel dining room in a small Bedfordshire town, I caught the charity bug. As I mentioned elsewhere, fundraising auctions are invariably tremendous fun, a welcome break from the serious business of Woburn and Pebble Beach where a small slip, a momentary lapse in concentration, may have serious and expensive consequences.

Guests do not come to a charity event looking for a bargain. They arrive expecting to pay over the odds and are happy to do so. (Most are, anyway; there is always a handful of miserables who glue their hands to the table and tut-tut at the sums their generous fellow guests are prepared to raise for a worthy cause; in our family we call such people "mouldy warps".) Punters at business auctions are stone-cold sober; those at charity dos are often a bit tiddly. The auctioneer can tease them and make little jokes, and a mistake, when carefully handled, invariably has them roaring with laughter rather than frowning into their catalogues (as is the case, understandably, in conventional auctions).

I am fortunate to have entered the world of charity functions relatively late in life. This has helped me avoid getting carried away by the glitz, celebrity and El Dorado-like wealth that hangs over many of these surreal events. I am also grateful to friends and family who have from time to time reminded me that fame and fortune are but words, and the things in life that really matter do not come wrapped in tinsel. No one did this better than our wise and kindly saleroom manager, Evan Willison. I will never forget how he planted my feet firmly back on the ground after my first major celebrity gig.

The event was one of Elton John's famous White Tie & Tiara balls. Every year, on the first Thursday in June, Elton and David Furnish built a monumental, themed set in the magnificent gardens of their house near Windsor. Everyone who was anyone (with money, of course) was invited and the headline act was always top drawer: Lady Gaga, Justin Timberlake, Kylie Minogue and, of course, Elton himself. The auction was unlike anything I had experienced before. The lots were not conventional items of value but money-can't-buy experiences. I remember selling an Audi decorated by Damien Hirst, a work of art by Tracey Emin, and the lot to end all lots, a chance to accompany Elton and David on a visit to one of their charitable projects in Africa. The sums raised by these auctions sometimes ran into many millions of pounds, all of which went straight to Elton's AIDS Foundation.

For my first White Tie & Tiara ball, a very posh car arrived to pick up Sally and me and drive us to Elton's estate. Returning to the office the following day, I tried to impress Evan by telling him what had happened.

'A chauffeur-driven limousine was sent to pick us up,' I boasted. Evan nodded his mop of grey hair and said nothing.

'And it had tinted windows,' I continued, 'so when we stopped before the gates of Elton's mansion, waiting for them to open, the crowd of paparazzi had to press their cameras right up against the glass to get a picture of Sally and me.'

Evan remained impassive. 'And?'

'And as we drove through, I looked out of the back window and saw them all peering into their screens and setting their cameras up for the next celeb.'

'They weren't,' retorted Evan.

'Eh? Weren't what, Evan?'

'Setting up their cameras for the next celeb.'

'So what were they doing?'

Evan, with a face as straight as a Jimmy Anderson yorker, explained, 'With all due respect, Charlie, they were muttering, "Who the hell was that?" and deleting the pictures they'd just taken.'

He was right, of course, and it was a salutary reminder. It is a mistake to think that because one mixes with the high and mighty, one is high and mighty oneself. The chickens in Bletchley market are never far away.

The most difficult venue in which I have had to auction is the Royal Albert Hall. The place is so vast that it's almost impossible to see the bidders in the higher seats, let alone hear them – unless, of course, they happen to be opera singers. The event was another organised by CLIC (Cancer and Leukaemia in Childhood) before it joined with Sargent Cancer Care for Children to become CLIC Sargent. I was asked to conduct the auction on a catwalk that stretched out into the middle of the vast arena. Surrounded by a wall of faces reaching high on all sides, I have rarely felt so exposed and, like a Roman gladiator in the Colosseum, I determined to put on a special show.

The opportunity came with Lot 6, a Picasso print signed by the artist with an estimated value of £25,000. So as not to frighten people off, I started the bidding at £10,000. Before long it had risen to £50,000, with two punters still in. The hall fell silent, hanging on every word. This was a real contest, a fight if not to the death then at least to exhaustion between the middle-aged wife of an inordinately wealthy businessman and a young Irishman. (I knew he was Irish from the witty, rather rude comments that accompanied his bids!)

Eventually, after many oohs and aahs, I brought the gavel down on an astronomical £200,000. The woman had won, leaving the defeated Irishman licking his wounds.

As the applause died down, I congratulated the winner.

To add a bit more colour to the contest, I asked, 'I assume you like Picasso, madam?'

'No, not really.' A ripple of astonishment ran round the hall and I sensed an opportunity. It was an old device but worth a try ...

'In which case, madam, having paid for it, I don't suppose you want to donate your new purchase back to the charity?'

To my utter astonishment, she agreed. More applause. I was on a roll and immediately set off to the other end of the catwalk where the Irishman was sitting. Despite his recent defeat, he looked remarkably chipper.

'Sir, this splendid print is once more available. Would you care to keep in your bid of one hundred and ninety thousand pounds?'

It was a long shot but my aim was true and it hit the target. 'Of course I would,' he grinned. Yet more applause. The hall hadn't seen anything like this since the Last Night of the Proms.

There was no stopping me now. 'In which case,' I continued, 'Perhaps it would be nice to round it up to the two hundred thousand pounds that the lady paid?'

He gave me another grin and agreed. It was all too good to be true.

'Unlike the lady who bought the print the first time,' I went on, 'I assume you like Picasso, sir?'

'Like Picasso, Charlie? No, I can't stand his work!'

By now the hall was in uproar and I had no option but to ask the inevitable follow up.

'Really? Then I suppose you want to follow the example of the lady who first bought it and donate it back to the charity?'

'Why not?'

I could think of lots of reasons why not, spending nearly

a quarter of a million pounds and getting nothing in return being one of them. I kept my thoughts to myself, thanked him warmly for his generosity and started again with the Picasso print. The picture with an estimated value of £25,000 had already made £400,000 and it was too much to expect it to bring in much more.

This time the bidding stopped at a more modest £75,000. Urged on by the crowd, I asked the buyer if he would like to keep the print.

'Of course,' he replied. 'That's why I bought it!'

CHAPTER NINETEEN

Boxers and Beetles

I am often asked about the most unusual item I've sold at auction. Thinking about this, I made a shortlist on the back of an envelope and the Odd Lot medal winners came out as follows.

Gold medal
After a photo finish, the winner has to be my friend Paddy Marshall, who ran a flourishing veterinary practice near where we live. At a charity auction to raise funds for the Bicester Choral & Operatic Society, he kindly offered the neutering of a cat. The lot raised more laughs than cash and I struggled to get the price up to a modest £50.00.

After I had brought the gavel down, I congratulated the purchaser and enquired out of interest, 'I assume, madam, that you do have cat?'

'No, but I do have a husband.' Priceless.

Silver medal
In second place is another medical man. I was about to start a

fundraising auction for the Retail Trust in the Grosvenor House Hotel, London, when I was approached by a distinguished-looking man in his mid-60s. I learned later that he was a leading Harley Street surgeon. He said that he would like to make a last-minute contribution to the lots: a hip replacement operation, excluding the anaesthetist or hospital fees. At the time it was worth about £7,000.

As we already had eight excellent lots, I hesitated. 'That's very kind of you, sir. But what if no one in the audience wants their hip replaced at the moment?'

'It doesn't matter. If it makes only one pound, the Retail Trust will be better off.'

He was most insistent and in the end I accepted this generous but idiosyncratic ninth lot. I sold it for £3,500 to a spritely man aged about forty. I thanked him for his winning bid and said how sorry I was that he needed a hip replacement so early in life.

'Oh, but I don't need one now,' he replied. 'It's insurance. I probably will do in about thirty years' time.'

'Thirty years? Have you *seen* the age of the surgeon?'

Bronze medal
In third place is a rack of used pipes – the tobacco type, not drainage. They belonged to Harold Wilson, the astute and successful Labour Prime Minister, 1964–1970 and 1974–1976. After Harold's retirement, his wife Mary, by then Lady Mary, became President of the Oxford Operatic Society (see Chapter Ten) for whom I occasionally performed alongside the Wilsons' son Robin. His parents were loyal supporters of the society and came to our performances whenever free to do so.

After Mary's death in 2018, Robin asked my advice about disposing of the contents of his parents' Westminster home. I suggested that I ought to take a look before suggesting the next move. He duly agreed and he and his wife Joy showed me around.

It was like being transported back into the world of 1960s newsreels. There was a whole rack of the famous pipes that were part of Harold's image as a straightforward man-of-the-people (he had been an Oxford don!) On the wall hung paintings gifted by the Soviet premiers Nikita Khrushchev and Leonid Brezhnev. Boxes were stuffed with handwritten speeches and photographs signed by a galaxy of well-known figures, including US Presidents and HM Queen Elizabeth II. Of particular interest to me (sport + silver!) was the hall-marked salver presented by the 1966 England World Cup-winning football team to Prime Minister Wilson when, to mark their achievement, he invited them to a reception in his official residence at 10 Downing Street.

Robin and Joy unselfishly donated most of the papers and other items of national significance to the Bodleian Library, Oxford. As well as political material, the collection included the correspondence between Mary, an accomplished poet, and her poet laureate friend, Sir John Betjeman. Everything else was to be sold by auction. Though I would have loved to value the unique collection, I had neither the time nor expertise. But I knew just the man for the job: David Fletcher, the meticulous scholar who had worked in our Woburn saleroom for several years.

The Wilsons decided not to give the sale to one of the large London auction houses but to the Derby auction rooms of my friend and colleague Charles Hanson. After the auction, Sally and I were honoured with an invitation to Mary's memorial service, where we sat amid a galaxy of the great and good, including the writer and media personality Gyles Brandreth and two former prime ministers, Gordon Brown and Sir John Major. The address by the former cabinet minister Dame Margaret Beckett emphasised the cruelty of unwarranted and unfair media intrusion, which Mary had risen above with great dignity. The singing of the choir, made up largely of family members, reminded us of the Wilsons' remarkable breadth of talent.

The auction catalogue was superb. Where possible, for example, each pipe was accompanied by a photograph of the prime minister smoking it! The other lots auctioned by Charles Hanson and me included a large selection of Christmas cards and letters from the Royal Family and US Presidents Nixon, Regan, Clinton and others, a baseball cap from President Lyndon B. Johnson, signed photographs of Pope Paul VI and French President Charles de Gaulle, a fascinating collection of books including Charlie Chaplin's autobiography (signed "To Harold and Mary, this is the best I can do!"), a bottle of Centenary HP Sauce labelled "The Rt Hon Harold Wilson MP" (Harold's professed liking for the sauce was another element of his man-of-the-people image), and a pair of Foster's De Luxe running spikes, a reminder of Harold's prowess as a sprinter in his school and undergraduate days.

The sale was well attended. Online interest was frenetic and just about every item sold for well over the estimated price. I had never auctioned a pipe before, let alone a rackful of second-hand ones. It was the sort of thing one throws in the bin or on the bonfire – but not when they've been filled, tamped, lit and drawn on by a prime minister! Like that they're worth hundreds of pounds, which is precisely what they sold for.

Odd Lots : Honorary mention
The boxer Frank Bruno was out of the medals but came in a good fourth after a sprint to the line against Harold Wilson. Frank is, as he's the first to admit, no artist and the self-portrait he entered into a fundraising auction looked as if it

had either been painted before he took off his gloves or was an attempt to emulate an early Picasso. Or both. Nevertheless, Frank is a lovely man with a huge following and I managed to get £10,000 for what was probably the least impressive painting I have ever sold.

Fundraising auctions like the one above take me to strange places. Some are humble, like one held in a tent in a field in Blean, Kent. Churches require tact ('the vicar is very liberal, Charlie, but it might be a good idea to steer clear of blasphemy'). Charging up and down stairs in a four-storey restaurant was undoubtedly the most physically shattering. I remember auctioning on the spinning top of the GPO Tower (now the BT Tower) in central London as my "vertigo" show, and the one in London's Natural History Museum, conducted beneath the skeleton of a gigantic dinosaur, as my "Jurassic Park" remake.

A couple of times I have raised funds for worthy causes from the centre of a boxing ring. For gentle folk like me, just standing in that blood- and sweat-soaked square of canvas is intimidating enough; being there alongside a World Heavyweight Champion is positively terrifying. But it has given me the right, when trying to impress my grandchildren, to say that I have been in the ring with Wladimir Klitschko, one of the greatest heavyweight champions of all time. When they ask who won, I say I can't recall …

Before what turned out to be his final fight, Wladimir predicted the outcome, recorded it on a USB stick and had it sewn into the sleeve of the robe that he would wear on the night of the fight. After the contest, which Anthony Joshua won on a technical knockout in the eleventh round, the former champion announced that he would have the robe – including the secret prediction – sold at auction to raise money for the wildlife charity he had set up. Helen

Fairclough, the event organiser, invited me to conduct it. I replied that, much as I would like to, that evening I was booked at a fundraising ball for Great Ormond Street Hospital.

Helen thought for a moment. 'We know you like sport, and we'd really like you to be our auctioneer. Where's the Great Ormond Street Hospital auction being held?'

'The Rosewood Hotel.'

'Do you think it'll be finished by 10 pm?'

'Should be, yes.'

'And are you up to two auctions in one night?'

Was she questioning my manhood? 'Of course, Helen. No problem.'

For commercial reasons determined by the need to attract global audiences, top-level boxing contests generally take place late at night, UK time. Consequently, there was nothing unusual in the fundraising part of Helen's gig beginning at 10.30 pm, allowing me to perform my two-in-one-night stunt. The plan went as smoothly as one of Klitschko's famed four-punch combinations. I finished the Great Ormond Street auction at 9.55 pm, said my goodbyes and went outside to find a car waiting to take me to the Royal Horticultural Society's Lawrence Hall where I was to conduct the boxing auction. On arrival, I brushed down my dinner jacket, straightened my tie, took a sip of whisky, and stepped onto the ringside rostrum.

The first few items went well, raising a healthy sum for the Klitschko wildlife charity. It was now the turn of the robe with its unknown prediction sewn inside. The great (in every sense of the word) man stepped into the ring to present the lot in person and guarantee its authenticity. To my alarm, he then invited me to leave the safety of the rostrum and join him inside the ropes. I have never felt so small, a Jack beside a Beanstalk Giant of 6 ft 7 in (2.0 m), 247 lb (17.5 stone, 112 kg). He talked very eloquently for a minute or so before handing over to me. As he stepped aside, he leaned down and whispered in my ear, 'Thirty thousand, Charlie. Thirty thousand for my robe. Please.'

The "please" was a nice touch. It made it sound less of a threat. I'm sure it wasn't one, but I couldn't help wondering, as I gazed up at that man mountain and muttered, 'I'll do my best,' what might happen if I let him down ... No pressure, then.

On occasions like this, it's tricky knowing where to start. If I come in too low, afraid of scaring punters off, it can demean the value of the lot and make it harder to reach its potential. On the other hand, a high opening call runs the risk of getting no bid at all, and I am faced with the embarrassment of having to back down to a lower figure. This sends out the message that the lot is not worth as much as the auctioneer, clearly not up to the job, thought it was!

I glanced across at the genial Goliath. Did I imagine him mouthing thirty thousand? Probably. Nevertheless, the figure was burned into my brain. What the hell – let's go for it!

'And now you have the opportunity to acquire a totally unique item, one that has never been seen before and never will be again. It's a genuine one-off: the gown Wladimir Klitschko wore before his fight with Anthony Joshua, with a USB stick sewn into the sleeve containing Wladimir's secret pre-fight prediction of the outcome.

'So, how about fifty thousand pounds?'

Yes! A hand went up immediately! I heaved a sigh of relief and glanced towards Wladimir. He was smiling broadly.

'Too cheap!' I cry. 'The gown alone is worth that. But you have a double whammy, gown plus that mystery USB. It's a priceless historical artefact! Who will give me fifty-five thousand pounds?'

A woman raised her hand, and on we went ... £60,000 ... £80,000 ... £100,000. In the end, the woman who had come in at £55,000 secured the lot for a massive and extremely generous £160,000. Wladimir was ecstatic. For a moment I feared for my life as he bounded across the ring, picked me up and gave me a rib-crushing bear hug.

I was exhausted and felt as if I had been through a mangle. But it was so worth it: yes, children, I have been in the ring with Wladimir Klitschko.

Boxing and golf are not the only sports for which I have helped raise funds. I've worked with rugby organisations, notably Leicester Tigers, for many years. An auction at a rugby club is like no other and takes me back to my time as a player in Buckingham. The beer and the songs are only part of the story. What really marks out the rugby world is the unbreakable sense of comradeship born, I imagine, from participation in a sport with a high degree of danger and physical contact. Arrogant square pegs, no matter how talented, do not fit into the round hole of rugby, the ultimate team sport.

Cricket, my principal sporting obsession, is also a team game. In my experience, the closest it comes to emulating rugby's camaraderie is in the ranks of the MCC (see Chapter Fourteen). I have conducted auctions for this prestigious club on behalf of well-known individual cricketers, including the late Shane Warne, the brilliant and ebullient Australian spin bowler. Though latterly struggling to come to terms with his celebrity, he was a larger-than-life personality whose warmth and energy made him a pleasure to work with. So too with his former fiancée Elizabeth Hurley. I had met her once or twice on the charity fundraising circuit (her presence always guaranteed a healthy – and wealthy – audience), when she called one day to ask if I'd run the lunchtime auction at a charity cricket match in which Shane was playing at a ground in the Cotswolds. The double pull of Warne and Hurley was irresistible. A successful auction crowned a most enjoyable day.

This led to an invitation from Shane himself. He was holding a fundraising breakfast at the Melbourne Cricket Ground (MCG) in aid of his Foundation for "seriously ill and underprivileged children and teenagers". Would I 'be a mate' and run the auction for him? The occasion was planned for the first morning of a five-day England–Australia test match. Breakfast was chosen because international cricket matches do not begin until the overnight dew has left the pitch, usually around 11 am.

I hesitated, unsure whether I could summon my auctioneering energy so soon after getting out of bed. Besides, Melbourne is over 10,000 miles away from our Oxfordshire home. I explained on the phone that much as I loved cricket and admired Shane's sporting prowess and charitable work, I was afraid that I wouldn't be able to …

Hang on a minute! I checked my diary. Yes, on the date of the breakfast, Sally and I would be in Australia, visiting our daughter's father-in-law. In Melbourne, too. I agreed to handle Shane's auction in exchange for two tickets for the test match in the prestigious MCG members enclosure. Fair bargain, or so I thought at the time.

A key prerequisite for a successful fundraising auction is that the punters have had an opportunity to loosen up with a glass or two before the bidding begins. The organisers of Shane's breakfast were aware of this and had laid on cans of beer and jugs of Bucks fizz beside the coffee and croissants. The croissants went down a treat, as did the coffee – some of those present had clearly had a good time the previous night. Partly because of this and partly because everyone was preoccupied with guessing how long it would take the Aussies to thrash the Poms in the upcoming match, the auction was tough going.

It wasn't easy being ebullient and reeling off my stock of auctioneer's quips a couple of hours after waking up, but I managed. I needn't have bothered. The Aussies are a blunt lot and their blank breakfast faces made clear that the last thing they wanted at 9 o'clock on the morning of a test match with the old enemy was some bald-headed old Pom trying to make them laugh.

In normal circumstances, lines like, 'Oh come on! If you've got 500 dollars, you must have 600,' bring a smile and a raised bid. Not that morning at the MCG. Instead, it was met with a shake of the head and a deadpan, 'Too right, mate, and it's staying in my pocket.'

It was like the game Jokari: however well you play, the ball comes whizzing back at you. Blood from a stone is a cliché, but in the circumstances it was painfully apt. The only person who saw what a tough time I was having and who did his best to come to the rescue was the British journalist, Piers Morgan. Time and again he raised his hand to bid, ending up with half a dozen lots he had no need for or any interest in. It was an act of kindness for which I will be forever grateful.

Later the same day, Piers featured in an infamous cricketing incident that is still talked about whenever sports people meet for a chat. He can be outspoken on occasion, and during the previous test matches of the series he had been drawn into a spat on Twitter with the Australian fast bowler, Brett Lee. Although he had just retired from international cricket, Brett was still capable of sending down thunderbolts. Nothing daunted, Piers reckoned that he, a very ordinary village cricketer, could face a six-ball over of deliveries from Brett without difficulty.

I witnessed what followed at first hand. Piers had been foolish to pose the challenge, but Brett's response was cruel and extremely dangerous. He did not bowl at the stumps but at Piers's body. Four of the six deliveries hit him, cracking one of his ribs. It was so unpleasant that I could hardly bear to watch. As the famous New Zealand cricketer Sir Richard Hadlee remarked afterwards, it was a ridiculous business that 'could have proved fatal'. To make matters worse, England were completely outplayed in all the test matches and crashed to an ignominious 5–0 defeat. I have never been back to Australia.

The MCG auction is a rare example of a fundraising event that struggled to meet its target. Normally the opposite is true. A case in point was the UNICEF gig I attended inside the cavernous Billingsgate Fish Market. The main attraction was a performance by Sting whose wife, Trudi Styler, was one of the charity's official ambassadors. The auction, tabled to run before the show, culminated in a very special prize: a personal yoga session with Sting himself. This was going to be fun.

I opened at £1,000. Immediately, two attractive and expensively dressed women thrust their hands into the air. Both were looking at each other and smiling. *Ah-ha*, I thought, *friends, obviously, and probably friends of Sting, too*. I have never been fox hunting and do not approve of blood sports, but the mood in the hall was positively tally-ho as the two bidders chased pell-mell after their quarry. As soon as one put in a bid, the other topped it. The rest of the audience joined in, urging them on. It was like being at Ascot!

Eventually, at £85,000, one of the bidders dropped out. 'No more!' she cried, 'Not even for Sting!'

The lot had been such a success that I went ad lib and asked Trudi whether her husband would be willing to offer a second yoga session. Yes, she was sure he would.

Again, I started at £1,000 and, as before, the bids poured in. This time the lot sold for £65,000 to the woman who had backed out first time round. UNICEF had rarely had such an unexpected windfall. Both winners appeared delighted, too. And who were they? One was the screenwriter and producer Jemima Khan, the other Elle McPherson, the Australian model, actor and businesswoman.

It's surprising what you can find in a fish market.

And finally, the extraordinary story of the eight-fold Beetle. At a function in the Dorchester ballroom, the charity I was auctioning for was given a brand-new VW Beetle Convertible. It was an easy sell and went for £38,000, some £15,000 above the list price at the time. Knowing the purchaser drove a Rolls-Royce and sensing the mood in the room, I employed the device I had used to such good effect in the Albert Hall (see Chapter Eighteen). Did the man who had bought the Beetle really want it?

'Not really.'

'So would you like to donate it back for me to re-sell?'

'Certainly, Charlie.'

The second time round, the Beetle made another £38,000. I asked the buyer whether they wanted it, and they agreed for it to be sold for a third time.

This went on six more times, five for £38,000 and finally for £25,000. In the end, the charity made £291,000 from the sale of a single VW Beetle. A world record, surely?

Yet again, I had had enormous fun and been overwhelmed by the generosity and essential goodness of my fellow human beings. However, the overriding thought running through my mind as I left The Dorchester to catch the train home was how lucky, how very, very lucky I was. After all, had things turned out slightly differently, I might not have been pulling millions, but molars with Uncle Mac.

CHAPTER TWENTY

Six of the Best

When I was very young, family sing-songs began with a stirring rendition of "JG knew my father/My father knew Lloyd George," sung to the tune of "Onward Christian Soldiers". And who was JG? He, or rather it, was our car, an Austin 8 with the number plate JG 47986 (or something similar). It was part of the family.

The Rosses were car mad. My grandfather Chief bought some of the first to drive on British roads, my father built and rallied his own, and Uncle Mac's Jaguars and Aston Martin were among the hottest then available. My vehicles have been modest by comparison, but I have admired and sold at auction many of the finest automobiles ever made. You will have noticed, too, that cars, old and new, are a clear theme in the preceding pages.

It is appropriate, therefore, to conclude with a few words on six vehicles that have had the greatest impact on me over the course of my driving and auctioning lifetime.

1935 Duesenberg SJ Speedster, the Mormon Meteor

This near-legendary Leviathan of a motor car has to be my Top of the Pops. Not only is it a spectacular piece of machinery, but it was the lot that, more than any other, launched my career with Gooding & Company. To have sold the most expensive American car ever at that time ($4.05 million in 2004) in my first auction in the States was an experience I will never forget.

And the car? Viewed from the side, it looks like a crouching lion. It leaps like a lion, too. In 1935, stopping every 400 miles to refuel, it roared across the Bonneville Salt Flats for 24 hours at an average speed of 135.47 mph. It was then the fastest car in the world. The distance it covered was 3,271 miles, the same as that between Boston, Massachusetts and London, England.

Power came from a massive 420 cubic inch (6.88 litre) inline, eight-cylinder engine. To give an idea of its size, if each of the cylinders was filled with beer and stood in a row on a bar for you to drink, you would fall over long before you reached the end!

The Duesenberg racer is not only the iconic American car of the classic inter-war era; it is also one of the most exciting cars of any type.

Austin-Healey 3000 MK III BJ8

I have gazed with unfulfillable longing at the fine cars I have sold over the years. Exotic machines that were special when they first left the factory are now burnished brighter still by their rarity. They are – and always were – beyond my modest means. With one exception: the Austin-Healey 3000.

A final iteration of the "Big Healey" (along with the Jaguar E-type, the young man's wannabe motor of the 1960s) came under my hammer at the 2021 Gooding & Company's Pebble Beach auction. The 1965 car had been immaculately restored by specialists. Clad in what was known as "Healey Gold", with fawn beige leather upholstery, it shimmered onto the stand like a dream ... a dream that took me back to my own MK III.

My goodness, how cool I was! As my blue three-litre sporting monster with wind-up windows growled through Bletchley's grey streets, heads turned, birds rose squawking into the sky, MGB drivers threw jealous scowls in my direction, and anxious mothers clutched their daughters' hands more tightly. To hell with those pesky A-Levels – in his Austin-Healey 3000 Charlie Ross had arrived.

Not for long. After six months, the blue dream, which I

had bought knowing it was in less than perfect condition, blew up, and I sold it to David Johnson for £500. The one I auctioned at Pebble Beach went for $190,000. If only …

Bugatti Type 59 Sports

Here is enough history to fill a library – and a magnificent motorcar to go with it. The 2020 Gooding & Company "Passion of a Lifetime" auction was supposed to be held in Somerset House, London. The original building, constructed by the brother-in-law of King Henry VIII, was demolished to make way for the grand neo-classical public offices where my maternal grandfather once worked in HM Revenue. However, owing to the Covid epidemic, the sale was moved to Henry VIII's Hampton Court Palace, an even more historic venue.

This spectacular setting for an auction on the banks of the River Thames needed to be graced by suitably spectacular cars. Step forward the jet-black 1934 Bugatti Type 59 Sports, surely the perfect blend of industrial art and mechanical wizardry? During the mid-1930s, the marque's furious battles with the Mercedes and Alfas of the world's Grand Prix circuits earned it superstar status. Remodelled as a sports car in 1937, it dominated all opposition. The following year, my car of choice was painted black (with a yellow stripe – a nod towards the Belgian flag) at the request of its new owner, King Leopold III of Belgium.

It was an ominous choice of colour. Not only had the king's less than careful driving led to the death three years earlier of his first wife, the much-admired Queen Astrid, in a road accident, but in May 1940, against the advice of his government, he surrendered Belgium to the advancing German army. Deeply unpopular, he was forced to abdicate in 1951.

Successive owners maintained this dramatic vehicle in its original condition, explaining the impressive $12,681,550 (the most ever paid for a Bugatti Type 59) it fetched under my hammer. Back in Somerset House, I wondered what the bowler-hatted ghost of my eminently sensible grandfather would have made of it all. As a careful driver of a Morris 1000, he would probably have been rather relieved not to have had the throaty roar of a Bugatti disturbing the quiet serenity of his workplace.

Hillman Husky

The Hillman Husky, an estate car produced in various forms between 1954 and 1965, was not a particularly special vehicle. The name "Husky" suggests it had been designed as a workhorse, and its performance (0–60 mph in half a minute) certainly resembled that of a horse rather than an automobile. It was produced by the Rootes Group, an under-capitalised British company absorbed into Chrysler after 1965, making the Husky a sort of epitaph.

So what is this ordinary, outdated little car doing on a list of five-star specials? It earns its place because the name Husky takes me back to long summer holidays, when my father raced a crazy Italian in an Alfa Romeo around the Colosseum in Rome (and won!); when we had to stop at the top of the Simplon Pass because the radiator was boiling; and when Stewart and I spent long hours infuriating our mother with hilarious games of "Crabbies and Crawlies" on the back seat of our sand-coloured Husky, top-heavy with camping equipment on the roof rack, as it toiled across pre-motorway France towards the Mediterranean sun.

Though the Husky was not the grandest of cars, it will always hold a special place in my affections for the golden memories it inspired.

Mercedes Simplex 60 hp

The Simplex 60 hp was hardly mass-produced: in 1903–1904 the German *Daimler Motoren Gesellschaft* (DMG) company manufactured just 102 of these splendid 9.3 litre motoring carriages. They were as robust as they were powerful, winning early hill climbs and subsequently completing numerous London to Brighton Veteran Car Runs for vehicles built before 1904.

Remarkably, four or five (sources differ) Mercedes Simplex 60 hp automobiles are still running. Outstanding among them is the model I had the pleasure of selling in 2024. The Gooding & Company auction was held at Amelia Island, Florida, where the spritely veteran was knocked down for a price in excess of $12 million making it the most expensive pre-1930 car ever sold.

Part of the reason for the staggeringly high price was the vehicle's pedigree. This was, I believe, unique. The Simplex had been bought in 1904 by Harold Sidney Harmsworth (later ennobled as Viscount Rothermere), an early enthusiast for automobiles and aircraft. Harold and his successors were so pleased with the purchase that it remained in the family for 120 years – far longer even than their celebrated newspapers!

Carspotter's footnote. Why was the vehicle named a "Mercedes" and not, after its manufacturer, a "DMG"? Because Emil Jellinek, a fabulously wealthy Austrian patron of DMG, insisted that the engines he paid DMG to build for him – and later the vehicles themselves – be named after his 10-year-old daughter, Mercedes. The name stuck.

Vespa 125, 1967

The Vespa 125 was my teenage passport to a brave new world. There was no bus service to or from the village of Great Brickhill where I lived, and the hill on which it stood was too steep for all but Tour de France cyclists. As a consequence, for the first sixteen years of my life I was almost entirely dependent on my parents for transport beyond the village boundaries.

Then came the Vespa. Less than a penny-a-mile to run, nifty and easy to drive, I could now go to the shops, pubs (other than The Old Red Lion in the village), and visit friends, male and – a new discovery! – female. Snug beneath my crash helmet and sitting wheelchair upright, I putt-putted around the lanes of Buckinghamshire into adulthood.

The Vespa brand also carries profound family significance. After failing as a supermarket fruit and veg inspector, in about 1966 my father was set up as manager of a Vespa sales and repair business in Dunstable Place, Luton. The mods and rockers (scooters vs motorbikes) era was nearing its end, making a venture into the scooter business a dicey move for all but the most astute businesspeople.

Astute in business my father was not. GrayMac Autos struggled on for a few years before going the way of all his other enterprises. But not before he had given me my life-changing Vespa 125. I have no idea how he paid for it, but I will always remain grateful for his gift of freedom.